Reporting Cultures on *60 Minutes*

This is a book about reporting as a practice of communication that is deeply cultural. The authors explore several ways reports are constructed and used by the media: some as officially prepared as when done by journalists; others as less officially done as by ourselves or others in everyday routines.

Examined in detail is a report about Finnish culture that was constructed in a segment of the television program, *60 Minutes*. This brings into view journalistic practices of reporting culture but also Finnish lay people reporting, American lay people reporting, with each reporting not only about their homeland but also about the other's ways of doing things. These other, every day routines, are also explored. This range of reports gives voice to deeply cultural dynamics which are at play in international affairs on such a multicultural stage.

Unique in its content and approach, this volume:

- Demonstrates how reports are constructed as deeply cultural forms, couched in points of view derived from one's discursive habits and their meanings.
- Analyzes reporting done in professional practice/journalism as well as in common social routines.
- Offers a way through the process that can move reporting on culture from a self-reflective mirror to opening a window onto another cultural world.

Scholars and students in communication, intercultural/international studies, sociolinguistics and related areas will find much to consider in this work.

Donal Carbaugh is Professor of Communication, Chair of the International Studies Council (2004–present), and Director of Graduate Studies in Communication at the University of Massachusetts, Amherst, USA.

Michael Berry is Docent in the Department of Philosophy, Political History and Political Science at the University of Turku, Finland.

Other titles by Donal Carbaugh:

Books:
Talking American: Cultural Discourses on DONAHUE
Situating Selves: The Communication of Social Identities in American Scenes
Cultures in Conversation

Edited:
Cultural Communication and Intercultural Contact
Narrative and Identity (with Jens Brockmeier)
Distinctive Qualities in Communication Research (with Patrice Buzzanell)
The Handbook of Communication in Cross-cultural Perspective

Reporting Cultures on *60 Minutes*

Missing the Finnish Line in an American Newscast

Donal Carbaugh and Michael Berry

Routledge
Taylor & Francis Group
NEW YORK AND LONDON

First published 2017
by Routledge
711 Third Avenue, New York, NY 10017

and by Routledge
2 Park Square, Milton Park, Abingdon, Oxon, OX14 4RN

Routledge is an imprint of the Taylor & Francis Group, an informa business

© 2017 Taylor & Francis

The right of Donal Carbaugh and Michael Berry to be identified as authors of this work has been asserted by them in accordance with sections 77 and 78 of the Copyright, Designs and Patents Act 1988.

All rights reserved. No part of this book may be reprinted or reproduced or utilised in any form or by any electronic, mechanical, or other means, now known or hereafter invented, including photocopying and recording, or in any information storage or retrieval system, without permission in writing from the publishers.

Trademark notice: Product or corporate names may be trademarks or registered trademarks, and are used only for identification and explanation without intent to infringe.

Library of Congress Cataloging in Publication Data
A catalog record for this book has been requested

ISBN: 978-1-138-19104-4 (hbk)
ISBN: 978-1-138-19105-1 (pbk)
ISBN: 978-1-315-64066-2 (ebk)

Typeset in Perpetua and Bell Gothic
by Apex CoVantage, LLC

To
Marjatta and LuAnne
Intercultural Dialogue throughout the World
Finnish American Relations in particular

Contents

	Prologue	ix
	The Research Team and Acknowledgments	xiii
	Praise for Carbaugh's Previous Book Cultures in Conversation	xv
1	Cultural Worlds and the Illusion of a Singular Text	1
2	"Tango Finlandia": From *60 Minutes* to Cultural Discourses	11
3	Cultural Discourses in "Tango Finlandia": Some Initial Observations (with an American Accent)	30
4	A Popular US American Discourse about Finns as Others	41
5	A Popular Finnish Discourse: First Impressions	54
6	Enlarging the Cultural Discourse: Coding Finnish "Quietude" in Everyday Contexts	66
7	Reporting Cultures: Moving from a Mirror to a Window	83
8	Communication Practices and Cultural Discourses: Five Basic Findings	98
	Appendix	102
	References	105
	Index	113

Prologue

This is a book about a common communication practice: reporting. In it, we explore several ways reports are constructed, some as officially prepared as when done by journalists, and others as less officially done as by ourselves or others in everyday practice. The materials in this book draw a wide range of reporting practices into view.

Our focus is on a crucially important kind of reporting practice. Journalists and travel writers are often asked to cover elsewhere, perhaps Afghanistan or Wales, Canada or Brazil. As travelers when returning from wherever, we are asked to say something about a place we have visited and its people. Or alternatively, as a foreigner we are sometimes asked, what is our homeland like? When the need arises, we produce reports about cultural communities, our own and others. In this book we ask: How and why do we do that?

Our main illustrative materials explore a variety of reporting practices from two basic sources. One is from the American television news magazine *60 Minutes*. We examine specifically and in detail how a report about Finnish culture was constructed in a segment of this television show. This brings into view a journalistic practice of reporting culture. Included in this report, however, are various kinds of other reports: Finnish people reporting, American people reporting, with each reporting not only about their homeland but also about the other's ways of doing things. This range of reports gives voice to international and intercultural dynamics. As a result, as we detail in the following, the picture of reporting gets complicated.

Another source of materials we explore is from the everyday practices or routines of people in the United States and Finland. With these in view, we observe how people in both countries watched the *60 Minutes* report; we listen further to how they reported seeing the report and what they thought of it; we hear how they would report about their culture in ways that are different from those reported on television; we observe further for years how what people say relates to what they do in the everyday social scenes of their homelands. In other words, we explore how the televised reporting cultures are inextricably tied to the expressive landscape of each homeland. By examining these reporting processes and the peoples caught within them through these various materials, we think through an elaborate, formal and informal form of communication, reporting cultures.

Note, then, that our main title is intentionally multilayered. At one level, we are exploring the act of *reporting about culture*, our own and others. At another, we are demonstrating how the reports are constructed as deeply cultural forms, couched in points of view that derive from one's discursive habits and their meanings. In this sense, we invite reflection upon *cultural styles of reporting cultures* as in American English, in Finnish English, and in Finnish. Another layer of meaning draws attention to *a journalistic style*, a tribe unto itself, in which reporting is done as a professional practice (e.g., Robinson, 2011; Zelizer, 1993, 2004). All are in view in the following chapters.

The specific televised broadcast that is of concern to us is a difficult one; it is difficult for several reasons. As we discuss in our second chapter, the slice of television we explore is possibly the most frequently rebroadcast segment in the history of the *60 Minutes* program. The topics mentioned within it span Finnish history, geography, social customs, facial expressions, language, and enjoyment of tango; they also span American habits of self-expression, customs of social interaction, verbal styles, and much more. Eventually we found the issues in reporting cultures to run deeper than the simple topics of concern—in this case, the tango. Although the surface styles of dress or musical fashion may be pinned to an era or age group, the ways in which one cultural view often reports about another is not. In other words, we are focused more on the deeper ways of reporting and how those ways presume something about cultural points of view. These serve not simply to frame issues but also to deeply render a way of living in the world.

The way we suggest understanding this process eventually is through a metaphor. We have found, after watching and listening to thousands of viewers of these reports, that most reports about another culture are in the form of a mirror; they reflect the reporter and the reporter's cultural view more than they say anything about the cultural other. We demonstrate in great detail how this is done. The habitual and routinized way in which this is done is difficult to capture simply.

The focal broadcast is difficult for other reasons. Some younger viewers who see the broadcast often react on one level to the visual imagery (e.g., styles of dress, specific activities) and see this as dated. Yet also when asked, viewers from both countries reported, so far as they knew, that what they saw was accurate. The estimate of accuracy between viewers from Finland and those in the US was not significantly different. But the bases for these judgments, the focal images, language, comments, were indeed very different. For example, viewers from Finland could laugh at some parts, whereas viewers from the United States laughed maybe at those parts but also at others. Eventually, for Finnish viewers the laughter may subside and turn to irritation, even anger, as was said by a Finn in the broadcast,

"That's not funny," at a point where viewers elsewhere were laughing the most. The segment did leave a negative "taste in the mouth" of many in Finland. This makes the segment difficult for other reasons. We wish not to further irritate those who are upset. Our efforts, however, require close inspection of just how the report resulted in these diverse reactions—from laughter to anger—so to understand just how the report is upsetting. We seek to work with a keen sensitivity to this variety of reactions, especially in Finland, and toward opening the eyes (and ears) to how this was done.

For many in the United States, their views and reactions went elsewhere. As the segment played with cultural differences between the United States and Finland, a mounting sense of astonishment was created, as we detail in Chapter 3. This involved a play with Finnish features, resulting largely in misimpressions about Finland, with strong overtones of a negative cultural character. This is difficult for us as authors, for how do we expose this process, offer something more productive, without offending our colleagues, families, and friends on both sides of the Atlantic? When considering such a reporting process—ours included—we write at times with an irritation, at others an embarrassment, a little amusement, and still at others with a deep anger. In other words, we not only share, but eventually explicate ways the report traversed this diverse emotional terrain. And the anger or bewilderment grew deeper once we realized how pervasive the dynamics of this case study carried throughout our worlds.

Our purpose throughout is to examine the intercultural and international communication process through which this occurred. We emphasize that the concern of this book, then, is not fundamentally about the dance and dress, nor is it only about television broadcasts or journalistic practices. Although to some degree these are our main concerns, at base we are concerned with reporting cultures, no matter who does this, no matter where it is done. By the end, in our final two chapters, we offer a way through the process that can move us in our reports from a simple use of a self-reflective mirror to ways of prying open a window or door to another cultural world. This is not an easy thing to do, but it is necessary if we are to move beyond our own cultural blinders to an understanding of others. Such understanding is essential for enhanced intercultural, interreligious, or other productive forms of dialogue (Carbaugh, 2013).

Over the years, we have studied these sorts of reports and this kind of communication process with varieties of people from around the world. Our hope is to move the process from a culturally sealed, habitual daily routine to a culturally sensitive and reflective critical practice. Our earlier works have done this—in some degree—with the popular and prominent talk of Americans as in *Talking American* (Carbaugh, 1988), in popular discourses of Finns (Carbaugh and Berry, 2001; Carbaugh and Poutiainen, 2005; Wilkins, 2005, 2009; Wilkins and Isotalus, 2009), and in other cultural discourses (e.g., Berry, Carbaugh, Innrater-Moser, Nurmikari-Berry, and Oesch, 2008; Carbaugh,

2016; Carbaugh, Boromisza-Habashi, and Ge, 2006). With these and the current study, our eyes have lit with satisfaction when we have heard from our co-participants, "I will never watch news reports the same way again." This expresses to us the move from the unreflective mirror to the potential opening of a window to a deeper, critical understanding. Toward that end, we seek to move.

The Research Team and Acknowledgments

The key collaborators in this research have been residents of the United States and Finland for long periods of time. Michael Berry was born and raised in the United States, is a native speaker of English, and has lived in Finland since 1975. He has a working knowledge of everyday Finnish and has taught Intercultural Communication in Finland at the University of Turku and its School of Economics for many years. His teaching about Culture and Intercultural Communication in Business has been honored as a "course of the year" in Finland. Berry's book, *American Foreign Policy and the Finnish Exception*, demonstrated how successful dialogue was possible despite the tension between ideological preferences and wartime reality. When Finland was the only European country paying debts to the US in the 1930s, the American government and media created an image of Finland as an honest country which other European countries should learn from. The positive image increased when Finland was the first western democracy to stand up against an aggressive country (i.e., Russia) during WWII. Finnish cooperation with Germany to survive against Russia raised questions in the American mind but never took away the government's dream that an independent Finland would become the model for cooperative democracy along the Russian border after the war. This moment in history contrasts with the materials in this book which create a different image of Finland. In both cases, whatever image is created in international politics via cultural discourses, each is always couched in often subconscious 'traps' for miscommunication. Our current book thus demonstrates how we can all reflect on ways to minimize misinterpretations of others and create a basis for movement forward. Like Berry, Carbaugh was born and raised in the United States and has lived in Finland for extended periods. Since 1993, when he and his family lived in Finland for seven months, he has taught at the Universities of Jyväskylä, Tampere, Turku, and studied Finnish while conducting ethnographic fieldwork in Finland. During the academic year of 2007–2008, he was the Fulbright Distinguished Professor and Bicentennial Chair of North American Studies at the University of Helsinki, Finland. Both Berry and Carbaugh have published works on communication and culture with special attention to American and Finnish dynamics, among others. For this project, a broad research team was involved in different ways at different times, with this considerable support acknowledged below. Carbaugh wrote this work with the ever-helpful readings of and reactions to it provided principally by Berry, but also others. Among those, Ritva Levo-Henriksson of the University of Helsinki, Michelle Scollo of Mount Saint Vincent College, and Richard Wilkins of Baruch College, the City University of New York, provided particularly helpful and detailed readings of an earlier version of the manuscript.

We are indebted to a large social network of friends, family, and colleagues who have aided this project over the years. In particular, we want to thank Marjatta Nurmikari-Berry (Turku University of Applied Sciences, Finland) and Lu Anne Halligan Carbaugh (Springfield Technical Community College, USA), both of whom contributed to data collection and analyses. We also wish to thank Saila Poutiainen (University of Helsinki, Finland) and Richard Wilkins (Baruch College, City University of New York), whose research and linguistic skills in Finnish helped in the early and ongoing stages of this project. Both of their research projects and reports on Finnish communication and culture have been helpful to us (see for examples their chapters in Wilkins and Isotalus, 2009). We also want to thank Pat Foley (Gallaudett University) and Karen Wolf Wilkins (Suffolk Community College, USA) for their work on the project in its very early stages. In Finland, we thank our colleagues at the Renvall Institute of the University of Helsinki, particularly Markku Henriksson, Rani-Henrik Andersson and Mikko Saikku, among many others; at the Communication Department of the University of Helsinki, Ritva Levo-Henriksson; at the University of Jyväskylä, Aino Sallinen-Kuparinen, Jaakko Lehtonen, Matti Leiwo, and Liisa Salo-Lee; at the University of Tampere, Pekka Isotalus, Nancy Aalto, Irja Pietilä, Pirjo Rasi, and Liisa Kurki-Suonio. Each of these Finnish universities has provided crucial support—financial, intellectual, and personal—especially the University of Turku's School of Economics and Business Administration who supported our collaborations in Turku during the late spring and summer of 2000. At the University of Massachusetts, Carbaugh is extremely grateful for students, colleagues and friends, in particular, a teacher of Finnish par excellence, James Cathey. We are very grateful for this support. We are deeply indebted to the Fulbright Foundation for funding our research in Finland during 1993 and again in 2007–2008. We further acknowledge additional generous support from the Finlandia Foundation National in the United States who provided Carbaugh a grant for this project. We are deeply grateful to all.

All chapters that follow were created for this book except Chapter 6. We co-authored an earlier version of it with Marjatta Nurmikari-Berry. It appears in the *Journal of Language and Social Psychology*, 2006, 25, 203–220.

Praise for Carbaugh's Previous Book *Cultures in Conversation*

"... Cultures in Conversation, *discusses the complex interrelationships among culture, conversation, and context. Through this discussion, Carbaugh highlights the necessity of deeper intercultural awareness and understanding as a prerequisite to effective communication. Carbaugh is highly successful not only in his endeavor to highlight the impact of culture on conversation but also in his illustration of the ethnographic approach to the study of intercultural communication. For those not familiar with nonquantitative approaches to the study of culture, this text provides a good introduction to one form of ethnographic analysis. The book can serve as a good accompaniment to any research methods course in psychology. In addition to providing an example of one form of qualitative analysis, the book is a necessary inclusion for anyone conducting intercultural or international research.*"

—PsycCRITIQUES

"... *the ease with which Carbaugh presents his arguments about culture and his conviction about his methodology leave the reader with the sense that there is intrinsic value to studying cultural moments, that more researchers should undertake this endeavor through his methodological orientation.... Carbaugh does not merely translate cultural moments for his reader; instead, he guides the reader through this process and makes them a stakeholder in its outcome.*"

—The Review of Communication

"*At a time when our contemporary world seems to be characterized and confused by reactivity, Carbaugh's book offers insight on the ways in which alternate systems of being, living, relating, and speaking take place in human interactions. Going beyond generalizations in exploring cultural communication, Carbaugh demonstrates the interdependence of culture and conversation through a rich collection of culturally situated encounters. His writing expands our imagination, stimulates our minds, and touches the hearts and souls of his readers.*"

—Ozum Ucok
Hofstra University

PRAISE FOR CARBAUGH'S PREVIOUS BOOK *CULTURES IN CONVERSATION*

"Cultures in Conversation *is another milestone in Donal Carbaugh's exploration of American culture as it manifests itself in characteristically American patterns of communication. The comparative perspective adopted in the present book leads to brilliant new insights into common American ways of speaking as well as the shared cultural assumptions and values reflected in them. Detailed studies of intercultural encounters, with careful attention to native labels for kinds of speech practices and cultural values, allow Carbaugh to identify 'cultural rules for conversation' from the insider's point of view, while making them intelligible to outsiders. The book also identifies some sources of intercultural miscommunication and negative cultural stereotypes and suggests some practical remedies for them as well as providing theoretical insights. Cultures in Conversation is 'ethnography of speaking' at its best. It will engage anyone interested in intercultural communication, language in society, and American culture.*"

—Anna Wierzbicka
The Australian National University

"*Whether it be exploring public discourse in Russia, learning to listen with the Blackfeet of Montana, or building relationships in Finland, Carbaugh writes with clarity and enthusiasm, quickly drawing the reader into the subtle workings of culture in everyday life. This book brings together some of his most intriguing work with new research and insights that give the reader a deep understanding of how communication, meaning, and identity are closely interwoven. In doing so, Carbaugh extends and elaborates on the theoretical implications of his work and an ethnographic understanding of the world. I have been reading and using Donal's work in graduate and undergraduate courses for years. The clarity with which he develops his examples and arguments makes his work ideally suited for students. I strongly recommend this book for anyone interested in understanding the relationship between culture and communication and the misunderstandings that are so apt to happen in intercultural contexts. For someone interested in understanding the ethnography of communication perspective and the insights it can provide, this is a must read.*"

—Bradford 'J' Hall
University of New Mexico

"*What Carbaugh does with great delicacy is show how culture is imbricated in the details of conversational practice. He examines cross cultural conversation because the misunderstandings which arise reveal the unusually unstated cultural understandings which the speakers bring to their conversations. Through this work Carbaugh shows how to link the detailed micro-study of conversation with the larger themes of social and cultural anthropology.*"

—Dr. David Zeitlyn
University of Kent

"*In* Cultures in Conversation *Donal Carbaugh offers a compelling and nuanced analysis of the many ways in which culture shapes moments of intercultural contact. His comparative accounts of the working of cultural codes in conversation invite readers to a journey of discovery of both self and other. The book presents a rich array of case studies of face-to-face*

PRAISE FOR CARBAUGH'S PREVIOUS BOOK *CULTURES IN CONVERSATION*

or mediated encounters in which cultural differences are puzzled over, negotiated and sometimes bridged, and thereby demonstrates how the nexus of communication and culture can be productively and systematically explored."

—Tamar Katriel
University of Haifa

"Donal Carbaugh makes an outstanding contribution to the study of cultural and cross-cultural communication through his detailed analysis of communicative practices in four different cultures. Using numerous examples of naturally occurring speech, gathered from the author's many ethnographic studies, Carbaugh demonstrates how the premises which guide communication can be discovered, described, and interpreted in such a way as to reveal how people create a sense of shared cultural identity. No other author has so clearly articulated the intersection of communication and culture as has Donal Carbaugh."

—Chuck Braithwaite
University of Nebraska at Lincoln

"Donal Carbaugh is one of our wisest analysts of culture and communication. Here he draws on his direct experience of Russian, Finnish, and Blackfeet Indian cultures to present a comprehensive and incisive approach to understanding conversation in cultural perspective. It is a perfect text for classroom use, but even the most seasoned researchers will find enlightening insights as well as delightful and vivid examples. I'll definitely assign this book the next time I teach Cross-cultural communication."

—Deborah Tannen
Georgetown University

"Donal Carbaugh's book, Cultures in Conversation, is remarkable. It is based on first-hand knowledge over a number of years of a considerable range of cultures and situations. The result is an invaluable contribution to understanding of communication and the ethnography of speaking."

—Dell Hymes
University of Virginia

Chapter 1

Cultural Worlds and the Illusion of a Singular Text

One experience from a time of deep political change comes back to me repeatedly. A few years ago I was lecturing in the Baltic state of Estonia not long after the fall of the Soviet Union. Our generous hosts had arranged for me and for my family to stay in a rather large apartment, the former KGB headquarters, close to the center of town, across from a small store. After buying some groceries, we settled into our living room and saw, against one wall, a large wooden structure. It was several feet long and almost as tall. In the middle of this rather large unadorned edifice was a small glass screen, about the size of a large pizza. Oh, we thought, it must be a television. We switched it on, and sure enough, after warming up, the screen began playing images that were accompanied by Russian language.

We had watched for only a short time when a familiar visage crossed the screen: a man on a horse was smoking a cigarette in a beautiful mountainous landscape, and we thought, yes, the Marlboro Man. As part-time residents of the state of Montana in the United States, which is the oft-presumed background for these ads, we thought we might even have recognized the specifics of the geographic location in which the smoking man rode his horse. I was thinking that must be the Rocky Mountain front to the east of Choteau or Valier. Yet as I watched the familiar landscape, an unease or perhaps even a disease welled up inside of me. Here we were in this nice country of Estonia, at the University of Tartu, near the Russian border, in the midst of much political optimism, exploring a deep intellectual history in semiotic studies, and what do we see but an American scene being exploited in order to induce people to buy—and smoke—cigarettes!

I was irritated by this. In a cultural and political world full of new hope for the future, our colleagues had been telling us in delight how the constraints of the Soviet order had been lifted. And what do we see now but a dose of Americana with a strong twist of capitalism, a consumer culture and its accompanying inducements. I wondered what my hosts thought about all of this.

The next day over lunch I mentioned the advertisement to my Estonian colleagues. I will never forget their reply: "Isn't that something! Now our airways are opened up to things we have never seen before. This is a sign of our new freedoms. We have access to information we have never had before." Yes, I said, but they are advertisements for cigarettes! "Of course they are. What does it matter? This is a sign of the changing times, of a better future for us. This type of thing comes with the revolutionary changes to our country." I would have never seen nor felt the televised image in that way—as part of a liberating cultural and political movement. But there it was: seen differently, felt differently, read differently into the social, political, and cultural features of this Baltic place. One image was on the screen, yes, but there were—in this scene—at least two deeply grounded, historically situated ways of speaking (seeing and thinking) about it.

Since that experience I have noticed similar dynamics on countless other occasions. Two years after my visit to the Baltics, I was in Moscow, Russia. A social conversation turned into a discussion about media personalities and the Spacebridge phenomenon, which had been prominent on television a few years earlier. We discussed two popular media personalities of that era: Vladimir Posner of Russia and Phil Donahue of the United States. My Russian colleagues asked if I had seen the one program when Russian teens were asked by Donahue about "having sex" and then the teens changed the subject. I said, "Well, yes, I did see that." As it had turned out, I had recorded and analyzed that very exchange as a part of a larger "cultural discourse of a spacebridge" project some years earlier. In fact, much to my delight, Professor Anna Pavloskaya of Moscow State University had translated parts of that research into Russian (i.e., Carbaugh, 2005). In it, the teens were asked by Donahue about "contraceptive use," "unwanted pregnancies," and "girls being virgins prior to marriage." The latter was prompted by the American host who had asked a young Russian woman about "sex"; she responded by saying it was good if a girl was a virgin upon marriage. So I had a detailed recollection of this televised exchange. After asking me about it, my Russian colleagues laughed (as I realized later they had read the article) and mockingly said: "Y'know, we don't have sex here in Russia." And everyone laughed again. The joke hinged on the common knowledge in Russia about what should be spoken properly in public, alluding specifically in this case to this exchange between Phil Donahue and the Russian teens. This had become a running joke in some circles, of Russian youth in particular, for it cast Russians—the youth of Russia in particular—as "not having sex," this becoming a complex cultural punch line about Russian self-presentation in public, the Spacebridge links, and cross-cultural exchanges more generally.

The joke runs deep, at least for some Russian speakers, as it is not just the silliness of the punch line that is at play in it. There are deeper cultural subtexts. All have to do with common knowledge of Russian life under and beyond the Soviet system. During this time, people knew they should guard what they said in public so as not to risk disrepute or damage from "the officials," "the party," or the Politburo. If they were to speak in public, they knew it was best to speak about things that resonated with predominant, collective virtues, especially those attuned with

CULTURAL WORLDS AND A SINGULAR TEXT

Soviet-political life. So, rather than talk about sex, unwanted pregnancies, abortions, it was best to say something about an ethic of proper family life, marital fidelity, and maintaining good relations among people. This deep dynamic in the punch line created a public scene in which speaking sometimes was humorous, since some ethical statements were made explicit and publicized, such as "we should be virgins," rather than others, which were oriented to the public statements of facts, "we have sex and there are unwanted pregnancies." The deeper dynamics at play then had to do with what was required or proper in the public sphere as cultural discourse, erected along political dimensions about collective virtues, government preferences, and enforcement agencies, with these being not only active in, but cultivated by, ways of speaking in public.

In this case, the Spacebridge phenomenon had been circulated as a cultural theme, a televised event recollected and turned into a culturally based discursive resource, a nod to past Russian life as well as a deflection of American life. All of this was done through a caricature of everyday practice, this turn of phrase—"we don't have sex"—not only to identify but to be entertained by a contrasting set of potent cultural circumstances, recent but also receding, in today's Russia.

Our worlds today are full of these dynamics. From Shanghai, China, where billboards of female tennis star Li Na tout traditional Chinese images with a Western twist of sport, to the Middle East where American ball caps and t-shirts announce American towns, to Mexico where Spanish, Mexican, and American dynamics coalesce. Each such image, from a moving to a still picture, to the ways of speaking about them, all are produced, seen, and interpreted from multiple views. How can we understand these various, globally circulated, visual displays, this variety of media, and how are cultural worlds active within them? How does one come to understand such dynamics as these in our symbolically circulated, multicultural worlds, as parts of our societies?

The study summarized in the following pages wrestles with these questions and addresses them through the study of cultural discourses, which are brought together in such images and through such processes. To explore these processes, we will focus on a prominent, popular, and potent internationally televised event.

VIDEO TEXTS AND TALKING ABOUT CULTURES: GENRES AND MULTIPLE MODES OF DISCOURSE

Here we introduce some of the focal concerns and issues raised in the following study as a way of sharpening our look at these complex multicultural processes.

First, the precipitating cultural text of main concern to us here is *one specific "news" program from television*, and the multiple discourses being used to produce, perform, and render it (cf. Zelizer, 2004, pp. 24–27). From "mashing" music videos, to rock concerts, to television programs, to casual jokes, many genres of discourse are widely accessible to people today. Each has its own generic form(s), and each can shape discursive life through its own stance. For purposes of our detailed analysis, we thus begin by examining one kind of text deeply from the popular American televised news program, *60 Minutes*. We explore intensely varieties of language and imagery that appear within that text itself. We explore this text, however, as an inextricable part of the cultural discursive systems on which it is inextricably parasitic. Just as the cigarette ad in its production and interpretation is tied to multiple cultural discourses, so, too, is this or any televised text. We explore it in this way.

Second, we are focusing on casual ways of speaking, both within and about this text, as these are used in *everyday genres of communication*. Let us elaborate a bit about this. Imagine you sit down in the evening, link to the Internet, and/or watch a news segment or program about a people or country unfamiliar to you. Then someone asks you what you have to say about that program or that country and what impressions you formulated based (in part) upon what you have just seen. If you decide to reply, you respond by formulating a report about that cultural scene, group, nation, or newscast. It is this process of routine communication, or reporting culture, that, in part, we seek to understand.

We are not focusing here, although we have elsewhere, on the special aspects of televised media (and cultural) literacy; nor are we focusing in this work on specific pedagogical tactics (although we discuss some briefly along the way). Issues of media literacy and pedagogy are deeply grounded in the study reported here, and thus we have written about them elsewhere, but in what follows our focal concern is in the everyday genres in and surrounding audiovisualized news—within a multicultural process. We are thus studying everyday discourse within and about cultural reports, and as a result we produce a report about a report, so to speak. In the final chapter, we turn to a more general, critical view of the process, that is, how we—everyday actors and journalists alike—tell cultural stories about others. We find, in the end, that such stories, through our everyday genres of communication, typically tend to say much, if not more, about ourselves than they do about others.

There is a specific communication practice in this which we explore, an everyday genre that is central to our concerns here. In every known communication system one learns ways of speaking in order to verbally present one's own "culture" to ourselves and to others. We focus here at times on data that involve "*presenting our culture to ourselves and others*." So, for example, when one is an American foreigner, as we often have been, one might be asked, "What are Americans like?" or "What is America like?". In response, we step into that genre and create with it. In turn, we might be asked, what is it like in Finland, in Australia, in China, or wherever we might live or visit.

When travelling or when meeting culturally different others, such a question is rather common. The response seeks to say something sensible about our homeland, cultural identity(ies), about "who we are" for others. Of course, there is always the option of avoiding a response or refusing the question. Many, however, respond, and we explore, partly at least, what is involved in crafting and interpreting this type of response from various viewpoints.

Speakers, then, can and do talk about "the other" based upon what they have heard and what we have said, moving the process up a level, so to speak, as they talk further about what we have said about their and our cultural lives. Of course, we can talk further about what they have said about theirs. It is this specific process of casting ourselves through our own terms and forms, and how others then use those accounts, that interest us here as well.

We should clarify that this type of genre—telling about ourselves and others—is focal not because we started this inquiry with questions about it. It is a focal concern here for several reasons: because it is so central as a communication practice in our globalized world today; because it is active in news reports generally; because it is in the televised program of special interest to us, as it is often in journalistic accounts; because reactions to this program are attentive to it and use it; it is focal furthermore because it is through a variation of this genre that this report you are reading is composed, as is all intercultural study or international reporting. There is much here to think about.

Third, there are crucially important *linguistic dynamics* in our analyses. The materials we explore have been produced first and largely (but not exclusively) in English, or more precisely, through cultural varieties of English. The televised segment was also later broadcast partly in British English, while also being translated and broadcast in Finland with Finnish subtitles. We are interested in these broadcasts, including the transition within languages (or dialects of a language), between languages, and thus in the interlingual dynamics at play within this process. We are also interested in the deep systems of meanings at play for each linguistic variety or in each way of speaking. We analyze these linguistic and interpretive dynamics by treating them as "cultural discourses" and "communication codes" (see later). This allows us, we think, to understand some of the drama among meanings that are at play within this prevalent global multicultural process.

From our view, then, we conceptualize this deep, meaning-filled process as a play of cultural discourses in which a single text is not really a singular entity at all. In fact, it can never stand alone, but is always already—in its composition and use—a different textual space relative to each cultural discourse, its variety in language, code, and expressive system. This plays out, we will see, through linguistic dynamics, cultural stances toward language, their meanings and uses, and the wider cultural philosophies of communication that are at play. Thus, this third set of issues brings together various linguistic and cultural dynamics from the vantage of communication.

Focusing on communication also brings with it a fourth set of issues. These involve matters of *interactional styles, focal images, potent phrases and their meanings*. From this view, we embrace linguistic analyses of language use, and yet we go further to expressive systems that include styles, visual images, intonations, interactive inferences, silences, and so on. To understand the communication of the process requires then a view of communication beyond language use, to the images employed, the sounds used, and the range of scenes created in the process. These all place language, its uses and meanings, in highly particular situations.

Images of the Marlboro Man, jokes about "a sexless country," ways of speaking about ourselves to others, hip-hop appropriations of American Indian images as done by the rock band OutKast, or similarly in German literature or popular culture, rock concerts in Ghana and Georgia, all are complex cultural and social scenes today. We will weave our way through only some of this complexity by focusing on a set of materials that has strong currency in two different cultural discourses. About it, and about such events, we raise the following questions.

The Cultural Study of Discourses: Ways of Seeing and Speaking

Our first set of questions is: How is a widely circulated text viewed and verbalized through cultural discourses? When people from different cultural worlds watch a text in which they may have some stake, what do they see in and say about it? We are interested, literally, in ways of watching and speaking about such a text. To pursue our interest we have not only listened to people speak in and about such texts, we have also videotaped people watching. Both have been very useful parts of our inquiry.

A second type of question we raise involves a cross-cultural comparison. How do the discourses regarding this text compare and contrast? What does each have to say (and see) that is similar, and what do they say (and see) that is different?

A third question focuses on the televised segment that we introduce later: Why is this discursive text such a prominent episode in the history of the most popular American news program, *60 Minutes*? What has made it so memorable and so powerfully remarkable to so many viewers? In the end, we will have something to say about that.

SEEING THROUGH CULTURAL DISCOURSES

We call the perspective guiding this inquiry cultural discourse theory (Berry, 2009; Carbaugh, 1988, 1996; Carbaugh, Gibson, and Milburn, 1997; Scollo, 2011). The main objectives of the theory are to discover, describe, interpret, comparatively analyze, and critically assess communication as formative of sociocultural environments (Carbaugh, 1990, 2007a). We use the concept "cultural" inclusively to capture particularly emplaced meanings people have made about historical, political, economic, and other dynamics. Within this investigative process is also the goal of developing a general theory from which to understand in particular cultural philosophies of communication. As an investigative procedure, it takes as its primary data communication in everyday life and as its primary theoretical concern a model of communication, which unveils the cultural features of those everyday practices.

Cultural discourse theory has its origins in the ethnography of communication (Carbaugh, 2008; Hymes, 1972), which stands at the juncture more recently of the theory of cultural communication (Philipsen, 1987, 2002) and communication codes (Carbaugh, 2005; Philipsen, Coutu, and Covarrubias, 2005). The perspective has been applied widely in several countries to many languages, including, as only some examples, the subfields of communication law and hate speech (Boromisza-Habashi, 2007, 2011), environmental communication (Carbaugh, 1996; Carbaugh and Cerulli, 2013), health (Carbaugh, 2007b; Duchan and Kovarsky, 2005; Suopis and Carbaugh, 2005), intercultural studies (Berry, 1997; Carbaugh, 2007a; Carbaugh, Lie, Locmele, and Sotirova, 2012; Hastings, 2001; Witteborn, 2007b), interpersonal relations (Fitch, 1998; Poutiainen, 2005; Scollo and Carbaugh, 2013), interpersonal pragmatics (Carbaugh and van Over, 2013; Block and Lemish, 2005), organizational dynamics (Carbaugh, 1996; Covarrubais, 2008; Hall and Valde, 1993; Witteborn, 2010; Witteborn and Sprain, 2009), and mass media research (Berry, Nurmikari-Berry, and Carbaugh, 2004; Carbaugh, 1988; Katriel, 2005; Philipsen, 1992; Wilkins, 2007).

The theory provides a systematic way of describing and then interpreting actual communication practices. Of particular concern in what follows, then, are, in the classic vocabulary of John Gumperz, culturally distinctive "contextualization conventions," which speakers see and hear in televised conversation (Gumperz, 1982, 1992). Some of these are identified and transcribed in detail in the following chapters. This attention to the linguistic and visual cues demonstrates the commitment in cultural discourse studies to detailed, descriptive analyses. But the approach goes beyond this essential descriptive analysis; it also interprets systematically what Gumperz (1982, 1992) calls "conversational inference." In so doing, it examines rigorously how specific interactional conventions of participants carry deep inferences and can do so—within multicultural encounters—in multiple directions. As explicated in greater detail elsewhere (e.g., Carbaugh, 1990, 1996, 2005, 2007a) and employed in various studies (e.g., Bailey, 2000; Baxter, 1993; Boromisza-Habashi, 2011; Hall and Valde, 1995; Wilkins, 2007, 2009) conversational inference, from the perspective of cultural discourse, can be interpreted as a complex metacultural commentary that is ongoing within communication practices. In the process, we decipher how culture talks about itself, as well as how cultures talk about others.

Through this program of work, we have formulated a way of interpreting this commentary as including "radiants" of expressive inferences, about identities (who is present and how they are related), about relations (how people are linked one to others), about actions (what is getting done now), about emotion (how people feel about the current interactive exchange), and place (how participants formulate where they are and the nature of things). The theoretical framework thus provides a way of discovering, describing, and comparatively analyzing culturally distinctive features of communication, then interpreting the distinctive expressive meanings that are active throughout interactional exchanges—like our focal text transcribed in the following chapter.

The approach is used further in subsequent chapters to identify the robust quality of these deep inferences as they are similarly active in various communication practices. In the process of analyzing these, we unveil how cultural discourses are active not only within our primary televised text and in the ways people discuss that very text, but are moreover finely interwoven into the communication coding of everyday life in its situated cultural contexts.

Our cultural model for communication study, then, suggests that television texts be understood as parts of cultural discourses, as being produced, and interpreted, from the view of particular, historically transmitted, systems of symbols, symbolic forms, norms, and their meanings (from Carbaugh, 1988, 1990, 2011; Philipsen, 1992). What we see, the images we focus upon, the language we hear or produce or focus upon, and the meanings of each, all are part and parcel of a cultural discourse system, a deeply rooted means of expression and its meanings. Formulating this system of expression is to explicate a cultural discourse and to identify its prominent features, eventually and partly, as a communication code. To paraphrase Ralph Waldo Emerson, we are only half ourselves; the other half is our expression. And thus we explore the cultural stances for interpreting our expressions and ourselves that are active in and about our lives. This is all we have.

Note, then, for purposes of this study how our perspective uses a "nested conceptualization." We understand cultural discourse to be a historically based *system* of words, phrases, visual images, sequences, forms, norms, and their meanings. To understand that system, we begin with a descriptive analysis that explores how a particular communication practice—such as reporting culture—occurs; we understand each as part of identifiable clusters of voices and forms. Next, we explore sets of clusters that create discursive meanings, then sets of meanings, and their inferences, their semantic fields, which are somewhat solidified in both the discursive production, and its interpretation. Our basic conceptual unit, therefore, is a part–whole relationship between a particular element of discourse such as an echoing sequence (in Chapter 3), and the larger cultural discourses of which it is inevitably a part (Carbaugh, 2007a; Carbaugh, Gibson, and Milburn, 1997; Scollo, 2011).

Some readers are undoubtedly familiar with other approaches to communication, conversation, and discourse. Our approach is distinct from but complements, for example, two well-known others, Conversation Analysis (CA), and Critical Discourse Analysis (CDA). Like Conversation Analysis, Cultural Discourse Analysis (or CuDA) is based on careful descriptive analyses of actual instances of social interaction, but unlike Conversation Analysis, Cultural Discourse Analysis not only identifies and analyzes, but also interprets the cultural meaningfulness to participants and comparatively analyzes the cultural features of conversational sequences. More basically, it conceptualizes its main concerns as cultural sequences. Like Critical Discourse Analysis, Cultural Discourse Analyses can employ critical inquiry, but rather than starting with a political project, it formulates the locus of critical inquiry only after careful descriptive and interpretive modes of analysis. As such, Cultural Discourse Analysis is a general approach that carves out specific empirical or analytical problems, which, when addressed, help decipher the cultural features in discourses, especially as these are at play in everyday scenes of communication. Interested readers might want to consult recent discussions about CuDA and related approaches in Berry (2009), Scollo (2011), and others.

A PREVIEW OF THE CHAPTERS

One frame colloquially supplied for the focal communication practices of concern to us here is a "news program." As such, the program is said to employ a journalistic narrative, or what one commentator has called when writing about *60 Minutes*, a "consensus narrative" (Thorburn, 1993, p. 1). This type of cultural story is one that has a deep history, which we will recount briefly in Chapter 2. It involves a special set of participants, specific plot lines, well-worn sequential structures, prominent normative elements, and their meanings. We conceptualize this framing itself as a form of cultural discourse—as it varies from place to place—describe it in some detail, interpret its range of meanings, and eventually, in our final chapter, critically assess its use in this case. Note then that we are treating a text of television news as we would treat technology generally, as part and parcel of cultural discourses. From this view, although any one text or medium might be seen and discussed within one discourse, no text can stand alone, on its own, outside of a cultural discourse, or outside of multiple cultural discourses.

Chapter 2 provides a brief recounting of the US American television program, *60 Minutes*, in which our focal episode was broadcast. The chapter also includes a detailed transcript of the specific broadcast, which we reference throughout the following analyses.

The case before us is indeed a complex one. In Chapter 3, we examine the discursive structuring within the televised text itself, revealing eventually that it involves a play between two cultural discourses. We create two concepts to identify this. To begin, we identify the dynamic as an "echoing sequential structure." And we find in the end that this form simultaneously activates different, culturally divergent, "parallel voices." That is, by attending to the text as an intersection of diverse cultural discourses, we describe distinctive cultural structures and forms that are operating within it, but not operating in the same way for the principal participants or viewers who are involved. Understanding this discursive structuring demonstrates how cultures are not only woven into this televised text, but offer different conditions for its making. It also demonstrates interactional sources of cultural inferences which are active in the discourse, yet are active differently, through different contextualization conventions, even at the very same moments. This leads to deeper questions that we explore concerning the utility of the echoing sequential structure itself, the parallel voices within it, and the larger journalistic forms being used to understand these dynamics.

In Chapters 4, 5, and 6 we deepen our analyses of the cultural discourses at play, focusing on how participants present their culture to others and present another's culture to themselves; this practice occurs both within and about the focal televised text. This type of reporting occurs prominently through what we call a "rhetoric of astonishment," as one reports how the other is somehow unusual and/or in need of some remedy or therapy. Presenting culture in this way functions to affirm the inferences one makes based in one's own discourse, but also often miscasting the other through the terms of one's own. This can be done in overt as well as subtle and unknowing ways. Our analysis seeks to understand this range. As a result, we can better see how talking about others often says much more about oneself than it does about another. It is this process and this aspect of journalistic narratives that holds our attention as we conclude.

SUMMARY

Our inquiry focuses on the ways our contemporary communication both presumes and creates culturally distinctive knowledge about persons, actions, social relations, feelings, and place (Berry, 2009; Carbaugh, 2005, 2007b; Carbaugh and Cerulli, 2013; Philipsen, 1997; Scollo, 2011; Witteborn, 2007a; Witteborn and Sprain, 2009). Following prior research, we are particularly interested in the ways cultural discourses constitute shared identities, proper styles of conduct, and ways of relating people one to another. Of special interest to us is a particular discursive dynamic, how discursive formulations about cultural others make the interactional other the content of expression, but, in the process, implicate deeper invisible forms from one's own culture. In other words, we will be examining how everyday verbal and visual representations about cultural others deeply reveal one's own cultural frame of reference, thus, at times, saying more about one's self than about others (Carbaugh, 1996, 2005). This is quite likely to occur in televised communication, especially in "news" broadcasts about others, in which portraits of cultural others become the driving theme and warrant for the programming (Berry, Nurmikari-Berry, and Carbaugh, 2004). And it is to one such program we now turn.

Chapter 2

"Tango Finlandia"

From *60 Minutes* to Cultural Discourses

THE *60 MINUTES* TELEVISION PROGRAM: CULTURAL DETECTIVES AND STORIES AT WORK

60 Minutes is the name of a television program that has been broadcast in the United States since September 24, 1968. It is referred to as a "news program" and is classified in databases in the genre of News/Documentary and Nonfiction. Based upon ratings, the program is the most successful television program ever broadcast. More specifically, the case is often made that the program is the most successful newsmagazine ever produced for television. After its first 40 years, the program has won 13 Golden Globe Awards and been nominated for 23 more; it has won 78 Emmy awards; it has the longest ever Nielsen Top Ten streak; and it is the only broadcast to finish number one in three decades. Throughout its tenure the program has attracted a large viewing audience, in the 30 millions per broadcast in the 1990s. Recently, the Internet Movie Database called it "the premier television newsmagazine (April 13, 2008)."

The accolades and respect for the program includes discussion of it as both the "the most popular program in primetime history" and "the most lucrative program in network history" (Campbell, 1993). Why has it been so successful? The creator of the show, Don Hewitt, says it is simple: the program has "narrative strength." He claims the formula revolves around one primary principle: "tell me a story" (quoted in Campbell, 1993). The "stories" have indeed been highly successful and are simply unmatched in attracting so many awards, large financial resources, and large numbers of viewers.

The basic format of each show centers upon three stories, three primary segments that are approximately thirteen minutes each. Each story can be understood metaphorically as a detective story, as an effort to capture the deeper truths and factual matters which often hide from the lay viewer (see Campbell, 1993). In the process, the reporters become featured in the narratives as key figures, as detectives who ask the tough questions and are willing to dig through the most puzzling of circumstances. The investigative drama can at times assume the quality of a "morality play" between "vice and virtue," with the reporter becoming an advocate for the common good. For example, when, before Monica Lewinsky, President Bill Clinton was publicly accused of an affair with Gennifer Flowers, he and First Lady Hillary Rodham Clinton appeared, of all possible places, on the *60 Minutes* news program. In the process, the vices and virtues of each political figure, and each as husband and wife, as well as their marital relationship, took center stage. In the end, the virtues of the participants at least momentarily prevailed over the pitfalls, for one heard little about Gennifer Flowers after this appearance. It seemed that, at least for a while (!), the unseemly incident had received its due.

Similarly, when a segment of the program presented the alleged heretofore hidden negative effects of the chemical Alar on apple products, there was an instillation of much public panic and fear. After that broadcast, my parents called me in alarm and said we should cease feeding all apple juice to our young children immediately! This story and subsequent reports resulted in a near public panic over the ingestion of apple products; but eventually a lawsuit was filed against *60 Minutes* by an association of apple growers, finally establishing the safety of their products.

Recently after his election, Barack (and Michelle) Obama granted *60 Minutes* their first public interview. And as one of its most gripping moments, parents of the children murdered at Newtown, Connecticut, discussed the urgent necessity for legislation of guns. The stories or reports of this program can thus gain the highest levels of prominence and visibility, entering into large-scale social dramas, political events, consumer decisions, and social movements.

This type of reporting can and has cut many different ways. Somehow, the programming, even the same segment, can appear conservative to liberals and liberal to conservatives. Hewitt argues this is so because the programming straddles a "fine line": "There's a fine line between show biz and news biz," he said in a recent interview.

> The trick is to walk up to that line and touch it with your toe but don't cross it. And some people stray so far away from the line that nobody wants to watch what they do. And other people keep crossing the line . . . . But there has to be a line because the line is called truth.
>
> (op. cit.)

And thus Hewitt argues that the stories must be anchored in the truth, to the facts as bases of news reporting, but also must somehow be appealing as part of the entertainment business.

Others wonder, as Richard Campbell (1991)—author of *60 Minutes and the News: A Mythology for Middle America*—has, whether the program indeed crosses that line. Some segments, according to Campbell, seem to feature detective stories that might emphasize the personality of the correspondent, the star detective reporter's cleverness and wit, more than the truth of the matter being discussed. Campbell discusses how the program is "the first TV news show to regularly cross the arbitrary line between news and entertainment by framing documentaries as detective stories, and by turning reporters into star performers" (Campbell, 1993). Campbell worries that through this process, the truth of the story is serving the detective agency, rather than the other way around with the detective agency in service of the truth.

This way of presenting the news with the reporter in the role of a prominent detective has, of course, worked quite effectively, at least as far as viewership and revenue is concerned. Massachusetts Institute of Technology Professor of Communication and Comparative Media, David Thorburn, puts the specific contribution of *60 Minutes'* to American democracy in this way: it is a mythologizing of America's core culture. How does it do this? The show, as we introduced in Chapter 1, provides a "consensus narrative," a phrase he uses to describe a group of stories that

> articulate the culture's central mythologies . . . an inheritance of shared stories, plots, character types, cultural symbols, and narrative conventions. Such a language is popular because it is legible to the common understanding of a majority of the culture.
>
> (Thorburn, 1993, p. 1)

From this view, the program cultivates a nation's myth, its sense of itself as a polity, or its ethos, including its treatment of its own political, cultural, and social dramas.

There are many insights one can find to be productive in these observations and much here to consider, especially when one group's "central stories, plots, characters, and symbols" are used to make sense of another. In other words, any "consensus narrative" or any group of "consensus narratives" may be used in the service of its own "core culture," but may also be, as a result, at the same time a disservice to others. In other words, any one narrative has its discursive and cultural boundaries and can be forced to draw others—at times in unfair ways—into its own purposes (Brockmeier and Carbaugh, 2001). As we have seen often in today's multicultural worlds, political processes, and global societies, when one detective draws the line around only his truths, drawing his understanding of others inside, considerable difficulties and misunderstandings can arise. Exploring some of these difficulties in action, how they are discursively constructed specifically, and how they are culturally tailored yet in different ways, all of this is at work in our consideration of our focal text, "Tango Finlandia."

"TANGO FINLANDIA"

While I was in Finland doing fieldwork during 1993, I got a phone call from the United States. As I recorded in my field notes at that time,

> [M]y parents called and asked me if I had seen the *60 Minutes'* television show about Finland. Of course I hadn't. Apparently, according to their report, the first few minutes showed "stern-faced Finns walking down a public street." I should try to find this program, they said.

I had heard similar reports from other friends and colleagues in the United States. Also, I heard within hours from my colleagues and friends in Finland about the program, who had heard about it from their friends or family in the United States. "Tango Finlandia" had begun surfing various cultural waves, an international process that was only beginning.

This process was initiated by the first broadcast of the *60 Minutes* segment "Tango Finlandia" on February 7, 1993. When returning to the States, several months later, I found a copy of this broadcast and began using it for purposes of teaching and research. I was surprised, however, when I heard repeatedly over the next seven years from various viewers about this segment. Knowing I was attached to Finland, I was repeatedly asked, did you see that broadcast on *60 Minutes?* Then from Britain, I was asked the same question! There are no public archives available for this period from *60 Minutes*, but by all accounts this segment seems to have been rebroadcast almost every year during that time. It was also, then, and later, in an abbreviated form, broadcast in Britain with a different brief introduction, as well as in Finland in Finnish. The shorter British version appeared on YouTube for nearly twenty years after the first 1993 broadcast, but was abruptly removed "for copyright reasons" in October 2012. It seems the broadcast has had considerable appeal, here and there, for nearly two decades! The segment has global "legs"! Why is this, and why has it traveled so broadly?

Without any further introduction, we will present a detailed transcript of the original broadcast segment. We have transcribed the text in order to capture as many of the qualities as we can on paper. Thus, the "*hh*" refers to out-breaths, the "?" to rising intonation, **boldfaced words** indicate vocal emphasis, indentations identify themes that elaborate an earlier less indented clause or repetitions in oral features. Lines were broken and commas inserted in order to capture natural pauses and cadences in speech. We have included for readers of Finnish on a line marked "a)", the Finnish subtitles used in the Finnish broadcast. (The broadcast, which is transcribed next, can be found at a password-protected site on Donal Carbaugh's researcher page: http://blogs.umass.edu/carbaugh/. The video can be viewed by entering the password TangoFinlandiaVideo1).

The "Tango Finlandia" Transcript

1) <u>SAFER</u>: ((narration, on camera))
2) with a good part of Europe going to hell
3)   in a handbasket, of *ethnic* and religious bloodshed? *h
4) last February we decided to visit a place where *
5)   if people don't exactly love their neighbors (.)
6)   they at least live in *harmony* with them.
7) Finland's the *place* (.)
8)   isolated by *language* and geography *h
9) where the national *mission* seems to be (.)
10)   to not be noticed
11) it's the most sparsely populated nation in Europe
12) It shares *hundreds* of miles of border with Russia?
13)   half of it is *permanently* dark all winter
14)   *all* of it *suffers* (.)
15)   from the permanent glooms *h
16) but a rich country. *h whose only excess
17)   is **massive** intake of alcohol *h
18)   and something else (.)
19)   that we'll get to later.
20) <u>SAFER</u>: ((Voiceover))
21) this is not a day of national *mourning* in Helsinki (.)
    a)   *tämä ei ole yleinen surupäivä*
22)   Finland's capital. ¿
    a)   *Suomen pääkaupungissa, Helsingissä.*
23) these are Finns in their natural state (.)
    a)   *nämä ovat suomalaisia luonnollisimmillaan.*
24)   brooding (.5) *private* (.5)
    a)   *alakuloisia, tuimia,*
25)   grimly in touch with *no one* ~but~ themselves (.)
    a)   *omissa oloissaan.*
26)   the shyest people on earth (.)
    a)   *planeetan ujoimpia ihmisiä.*
27)   depressed and proud of it (.)
    a)   *ylpeitä masentuneisuudestaan.*
28) We found that *no one* (.) looks *anyone* (.) in the eye (.)
    a)   *kukaan ei katso toista silmiin*
29)   so intensely private (.)
    a)   *he ovat niin varautuneita*
30)   that to be noticed (.) is an embarrassment (.)
    a)   *että on häpeä tulla huomatuksi*

31) to take notice (.) an affront (.)
   a) *huomion kiinnittäminen on loukkaavaa.*
32) it's *no* surprise (.)
33) that Finland has one of the lowest birth rates (.)
   a) *Suomessa on alhainen syntyvyys*
34) and one of the highest suicide rates (.)
   a) *ja korkeat itsemurhaluvut*
35) a nation of Garbos
   a) *He ovat kuin Garboja*
36) they all *vant* or *want* to be alone (.5)
   a) *Kaikki haluavat olla yksin*
37) isolated by *arctic* geography (.)
   a) *He ovat maantieteellisesti eristäytyneitä*
38) and a language of alphabet soup ? (.)
   a) *ja heidän kielensä on aakkosista*
39) gone crazy.
   a) *sekaisin.*
40) KNUTAS: ((Cut to Interview))
41) we're a silent (.) brooding *hh
   a) *Olemme hiljaisia ja alakuloisia*
42) people we think a lot
   a) *Mietiskelemme paljon.*
43) we like to ((lip smack)) keep our privacy *h
   a) *Haluamme olla omissa oloissamme*
44) and give (.5)
45) the fellow man (.5)
46) his privacy
47) keep a distance.
   a) *ja pysyä muista etäällä.*
48) SAFER: (Voiceover)
49) Jan Knutas is a Finnish author and producer for the
   a) *John Knutas on suomalainen käsikirjoittaja ja toimittaja.*
50) government radio service *hh
51) Finns, he says (.)
   a) *Hän kertoo, että suomalaisten*
52) have a difficult time making even
   a) *on vaikea*
53) the most *casual*? social contact *h
   a) *puhua*
54) with a stranger on a bus for example.
   a) *vieraiden kanssa*
55) KNUTAS: ((Cut to Interview))

56) I begin to think that *hhh
    a)   *Ajattelen, että*
57) I hope (.5)
58)   the other person doesn't say something ~I
    a)   *kunpa tuo toinen ei huomaisi minua*
59)   I might have to engage in a
60)   conversation now *hhhh hh
    a)   *Olisi pakko puhua*
61) it's (.) it's a horrifying thought
    a)   *Ajatus pelottaa*
62)   and sometimes you have to~
    a)   *Ja joskus on pakko puhua*
63) (Footage of Knutas and Safer)
64) <u>KNUTAS</u>: he actually says that *hhh
    a)   *Hän voi kysyä:*
65)   where are you going *h
    a)   *"Minne menet?"*
66) And then it's oh god I have to talk now *hhh
    a)   *Ajattelen:"Luoja, on pakko puhua."*
67)   even if I would like to say (.)
    a)   *Haluaisin sanoa*
68)   please leave me alone
69)   and let me brood for an hour *hhhhh uhhh
    a)   *että anna minun murjottaa.*
70) aaaa I'm too polite to do that, so I go along (1)
    a)   *En voi, koska olen kohtelias.*
71)   and get irritated in the process.
    a)   *Siis puhun ja ärsyynnyn samalla.*
72) <u>SAFER</u>: ((Voiceover))
73) Finns glory in their isolation (.)
    a)   *Suomalaiset ylpeilevät eristäytyneisyydellään.*
74)   Though they **claim** jolly Santa as a Finn ?
    a)   *He väittävät iloista joulupukkia suomalaiseksi*
75)   they take their pleasures **painfully** (.)
    a)   *mutta nautiskelevat kivuliaasti.*
76) the sauna is a **Finnish** invention *h
    a)   *Sauna on suomalainen keksintö.*
77) their favorite composer is their own? (.)
    a)   *Heidän lempisäveltäjänsä on suomalainen*
78)   Jan Sibelius (.)
    a)   *Jean Sibelius*
79)   whose arctic features (.)

       a) *jonka arktiset piirteet*
80)   are a guidebook to the national character.
       a) *kuvaavat kansallista luonnetta.*
81) SCHULTZ ((Cut to interview))
82) you don't read in the Finnish travel books
       a) *Matkaoppaissa ei kerrota,*
83)   that people don't (.)
       a) *että suomalaiset*
84)   like to **talk** and so *hhh
       a) *eivät pidä puhumisesta.*
85) even all all my *little~research~before~I~moved*~to~Finland~
       a) *Ennen tänne tuloani en tiennyt*
86) I~didn't~know~that~nobody~would~want~to~talk~to~me
       a) *että kanssani ei juteltaisi*
87) <u>SAFER</u>: ((Voiceover))
88) Teri Schultz is an American reporter *h
       a) *Amerikkalainen toimittaja Teri Schulz*
89)   who's lived in Helsinki for three years
       a) *on asunut Helsingissä kolme vuotta.*
90) Even though she now speaks the language (.)
       a) *Vaikka hän puhuukin suomea,*
91) the **ice** has yet to be broken.
       a) *keskustelua ei ole helppo aloittaa.*
92) SAFER: ((Cut to interview))
93) They resist even shaking hands?
       a) *He eivät suostu kättelemäänkään.*
94) <u>SCHULTZ</u>: oh my yeah definitely *h I wonder yeah
       a) *Eivät todellakaan.*
95) Shaking hands I think is~is~is pretty intense for them
       a) *Kättelyllä on heille paljon painoarvoa.*
96) But try to hug a Finn (h)
       a) *Mutta yritäpä halata suomalaista.*
97) if you've ever tried to hug a Finn, they're very **ugherr** (.)
98)   very (.5) shaky.
       a) *Siitä he järkyttyvät.*
99) <u>SAFER</u>: ((Voiceover))
100) even Arya Koriseva
       a) *Jopa Arja Koriseva,*
101)   a Finnish songstress and hardly a **wall**flower (.)
       a) *suomalainen laulaja ja kaikkea muuta kuin ujo,*
102)   is **comfortable** in Finland's icy reserve
       a) *nauttii suomalaisten jäisestä varauksellisuudesta.*

103) <u>KORISEVA</u> *(((Cut to interview))*
104) we have like a **wall** here
    a) *Meillä on tässä seinä.*
105) We try to *hh look at you and (.5)
106)   watch~wh(h)o~y(h)ou~a(h)re~
107)   w(h)hat~y(h)ou~(h)are (laughing)
    a) *Me tarkkailemme sinua*
108) before we dare to come to you and *h
    a) *Ennen kuin uskaltaudumme*
109)   speak with you (.)
    a) *puhumaan.*
110) and I guess the American people (.5)
111)   are more like (.5)
    a) *Amerikkalaiset sanovat:*
112)   **hi(.) who are you. where are you from.**
    a) *"Hei, kukas sinä olet?"*
113)   nice meeting you. I love you
    a) *"Hauska tavata. minä rakastan sinua."*
114)   (hhhhhhh) ((loud laughter))
115) ((Footage of Safer and Knutas))
116) <u>SAFER</u>: it strikes me uh traveling around this country that (.)
    a) *Olen matkustellut täällä*
117) people are **terribly** shy (.)
118)   particularly **the men**
    a) *ja etenkin miehet vaikuttavat ujoilta.*
119) <u>KNUTAS</u>: ((Voiceover))
120) among ourselves
121)   we think that is the natural way to be.
    a) *Ajattelemme, että on luontevaa*
122)   not to sort of (.)stick out
    a) *olla erottumatta joukosta.*
123) It's easy to see that from coming from another country *hh
    a) *Muualta tulevat*
124) you think of it as shyness
    a) *pitävät sitä ujoutena*
125)   and it probably is *yes*
    a) *Sitä se varmaankin on*
126) *((Footage of person purchasing tickets for a dance; Safer))*
127) <u>SAFER</u>: *((Voiceover))*
128) so what do they do about this clinical shyness (.)
    a) *Mitä he tekevät sairaalloiselle ujoudelleen*
129)   this almost **terminal** melancholy? (.1)

"TANGO FINLANDIA"

      a)   *ja alakuloudelleen?*
130) they come to places like this=
      a)   *He tulevat tällaisiin paikkoihin*
131) there are 2,000 of them in the country
      a)   *joita on maassa noin 2000*
132)   pay their **50** markkas
      a)   *ja maksavat 50 markaaa*
133)   that's about $12
134) and take part in
      a)   *ja ottavat osaa*
135)   what **has become**
136)   a kind of **national** obsession (.2)
      a)   *kansalliseen pakkomielteeseen.*
137) **the tango** ((Safer: brow raise))
      a)   *Tangoon.*
138) *((Footage of Finns dancing the tango in various places (10)))*
139) <u>SAFER</u>: ((Voiceover))
140) It's difficult to understand and **impossible** to exaggerate
141)   the importance of this *"***tango finlandia***"* (.8)
      a)   *Suomalaisen tangon merkitystä on vaikea ymmärtää ja liioitella. (both sentences 140 and 141)*
142) It can come upon a Finn anytime anywhere
      a)   *Suomalainen saatta ryhtyä tanssimaan koska vain*
143)   in the street (.3)
      a)   *kadulla*
144)   in the forests
      a)   *ja metsissä,*
145) which cover nine tenths of the **country** (5)
      a)   *jotka kattavat 9/10 maasta*
146) and on **public** holidays
      a)   *Yleisinä vapaapäivinä*
147)   **official fun** days as they're called?
      a)   *eli virallisina juhlapäivinä*
148)   tens of **thousands** will **tango** together (10)
      a)   *kymmenettuhannet tanssivat tangoa.*
149) tango halls are **everywhere**
      a)   *Tangohalleja on kaikkialla*
150)   for the lunchtime crowd on Helsinki's
      a)   *Lounasaikana tanssitaan Helsingin*
151)   most~fashionable~avenue?
      a)   *hienoimmalla kadulla*
152)   the **Mannerheiminkatu**(.5)

       a)   *Mannerheimintiellä.*
153) and to tango the night **away**?
       a)   *Tanssijoille löytyy*
154)   there are halls in the deep, deep woods
       a)   *halleja jopa syvältä metsän kätköistä.*
155) all the halls have one thing in common. (.)
       a)   *Halleja yhdistää yksi asia.*
156)   a sign like **this one**. (.)
       a)   *Tällainen kyltti*
157) ((Footage of sign with lit-up portion reading 'Miesten Haku'))
158)   it is a **shield** against **shyness**
       a)   *Se suojaa ujoudelta*
159)   it indicates when it is **ok**
       a)   *Siitä näkee,*
160)   for man to ask a woman? to dance (.)
       a)   *koska on miehen vuoro hakea naista*
161)   and vice versa (2)
       a)   *ja päinvastoin.*
162) for a nation that finds shaking hands
       a)   *kansakunnalle, jolle kättely*
163)   an overly intimate ordeal? (.2)
       a)   *on intiimi tapahtuma*
164) just imagine the **terror**
165)   of touching a stranger's waist
166)   or **shoulder**
       a)   *on vieraan vyötärön tai olkapään kosketus silkkaa kauhua* (sentences 164–166)
167) but the **tango** and this flashing light.
       a)   *tangosta ja vilkkuvasta lampusta*
168)   have become the official license to **touch**.(.)
       a)   *on tullut virallinen lupa koskea*
169) the **music** and **that illuminated word** say it all.
       a)   *musiikki ja valaistu kyltti kertovat kaiken.*
170)   not a **further word** need be said.
       a)   *Sanoja ei kaivata.*
171) ((Footage of Schultz))
172) <u>SCHULTZ</u>: it's **all** accepted within these=
       a)   *Kaikki on hyväksyttyä*
173)   these very **strict** parameters of=
       a)   *tiukkojen*
174)   of Finnish social **being**
       a)   *sosiaalisten rajojen puitteissa*

175) and um they don't have to **think**=
    a)   *tanssijoiden ei tarvitse ajatella,*
176)   they don't have to **think** of what to do next.
    a)   *mitä seuraavaksi.*
177) I mean they don't have to
178)   be **spontaneous** and it's not uh
    a)   *Oma-aloitteisuutta ei kaivata*
179)   **overtly sexy**?= which is something
    a)   *eikä tango ole liian seksikästä*
180)   they're very **afraid** of? and
    a)   *koska sitä he kammoavat.*
181) so it's it's all very well defined for them.
    a)   *Kaikki on tarkkaan määriteltyä.*
182) ((Footage from the tango dance hall))
183) <u>SAFER</u>: ((*Voiceover*))
184) there are strict **rules** to Finnish tango
    a)   *Suomalaisessa tangossa on tiukat säännöt.*
185) KNUTAS: the women stand on one side as you've seen
    a)   *Naiset seisovat toisella puolella*
186) the men stand on the other
    a)   *ja miehet toisella*
187) SAFER ((Voiceover))
188) **the men** (.)
189) for **them** (.)
    a)   *Miehet*
190) there is an **unwritten** code of behavior.
    a)   *seuraavat kirjoittamatonta käyttäytymissääntöä.*
191) KNUTAS: ((Voiceover))
192) it's **good** (.)
    a)   *On hyvä,*
193)   if the man is *h sober enough *h
    a)   *jos mies on tarpeeksi selvin päin*
194)   to be able to *h make half of the dance steps
    a)   *jotta hän selviytyy tanssiaskelista*
195)   and *h not step on the woman's feet too much.
    a)   *eikä tallo liikaa naisen varpaille*
196) ((Footage of Knutas and Safer))
197) <u>KNUTAS</u>: he should not (.)
    a)   *Hän ei saisi*
198)   smell of vomit or anything
    a)   *haista oksennukselle*
199) ((Footage of Safer laughing)) (.2)

200)   and then (.)
201) he should not sort of try to
   a)   *Mies ei saa*
202)   impose himself on the woman.
   a)   *tyrkyttää itseään.*
203) he=he shouldn't make the woman feel uneasy
   a)   *Naisella pitää olla turvallinen olo*
204) he=he should be the perfect gentleman
   a)   *Miehen on oltava täydellinen herrasmies.*
205) ((Footage from a dance hall)) (8)
206) <u>SAFER</u>: ((Voiceover)
207) the corners of tango halls look like handbag **heaven** ? (.)
   a)   *Tangohallien nurkat ovat käsilaukkujen paratiiseja.*
208) it reflects more the basic **honesty** of **Finns** than
   a)   *Se on osoitus suomalaisten rehellisyydestä,*
209)   wild (.) girlish (.) abandon. (4)
   a)   *ei tyttömäisestä huolettomuudesta.*
210) the Finnish tango. (.)
   a)   *Suomalaista tangoa*
211)   is not to be confused with the ***groin*** (.)
   a)   *ei saa sotkea*
212)   grinding (.) passionate (.) Latin American version.
   a)   *villiin latinalais-amerikkalaiseen*
213) the Finns have managed to **neutralize** all **that**. (.1)
   a)   *Suomalaiset ovat onnistuneet karsimaan intohimon pois.*
214)   it's a sad shuffle (.)
   a)   *Kyse on laahavasta mollilajin tanssista*
215)   in a minor key.
216)   with **lyrics** to reaffirm a couple's **instinctive** sense (.)
217)   of hopelessness.
   a)   *ja sanoitukset vahvistavat parin toivottomuuden tunnetta.*
218) HAKASALO ((Finnish Tango Historian/ Judge; Voiceover))
219) Lyrics is very hhh important because (.2)
   a)   *Sanoitukset ovat tärkeitä.*
220)   the stories are quite *sad* hhh and
   a)   *Tarinat ovat surullisia*
221)   and **melancholy** stories.
   a)   *ja alakuloisia.*
222) ((Footage of Hakasalo and Safer))
223) and they are hhh they are (.)
224)   **necessary** to Finnish people.
   a)   *Suomalaiset ihmiset tarvitsevat sellaista.*

225) ((Hakasalo eye gaze at Safer and head nod))
226) SAFER: ((Voiceover))
227) Ilpo Hakasalo is Finland's **renowned** historian of tango
    a)   *Ilpo Hakasalo on tangohistoroitsija*
228)   and the nation's leading tango **judge**.
    a)   *ja maan johtava tangotuomari.*
229) an **upbeat** tango he says?
    a)   *Iloista tangoa*
230)   is **unthinkable**. (.)
    a)   *ei voisi kuvitella.*
231)   no one would understand it.
    a)   *Sitä ei ymmärtäisi kukaan.*
232)   it might as well be **Japanese.**
    a)   *Sanat voisivat olla vaikka japania.*
233) ((Cut to Hakasalo and Safer interview))
234) SAFER: why this sadness?
    a)   *Miksi tämä surullisuus*
235) HAKASALO: because er::: (.)
236) we **are** um::er
    a)   *Suomalaiset*
237)   very melancholy hh people here in Finland (1.2)
    a)   *ihmiset ovat erittäin surumielisiä*
238) SAFER: and that?-
    a)   *Ja?*
239) HAKASALO: and **we need that** (.5)
    a)   *Ja me tarvitsemme sitä.*
240) SAFER: Is it beyo:nd? just melancholy
    a)   *Onko se vain alakuloisuutta?*
241) is it **pessimistic** in the sense that
    a)   *Onko se pessimististä, kuten*
242)   there will really be not much of a future for me (.5)
    a)   *"minulla ei ole tulevaisuutta?"*
243) HAKASALO: perhaps it is not **totally** pessimistic, but (.)
    a)   *Se ei ole täysin pessimististä.*
244) very many of the er er **stor**ies
245)   in the songs *h er (.)
    a)   *Monet laulujen tarinat*
246)   of course? they are **love** songs.
    a)   *ovat rakkaustarinoita.*
247) but er the **most** popular item is **love** that is o:ver
    a)   *Mutta teemana on usein kuihtunut rakkaus*
248)   or love that you are **still wai**:ting

     a)   *tai rakkaus, jota edelleen odottaa,*
249)   and you have waited that for 20 last years,
     a)   *ja on odottanut jo 20 vuotta.*
250)   *h and you are *al*most sure that it never will come.
     a)   *Sitä rakkautta tuskin tulee.*
251) Safer: (hh)   (hhhhh)
252) ((Footage of Knutas and Safer))
253) <u>KNUTAS</u>: The Finnish (.) male (.)
     a)   *Suomalainen mies*
254)   is very prone to-erm self-pity
     a)   *on taipuvainen itsesääliin.*
255)   *hh er::so: we have a lot of
256)   tango songs for instance which (.)
257)   er are written by males.(.)
     a)   *Joten monien tangojen kirjoittajat ovat miehiä. (sentences 255–257)*
258) <u>SAFER</u>: what are the stories?=
     a)   *Mitä tarinat käsittelevät?*
259) <u>KNUTAS</u>: sorrow. sorrow. sorrow.=
     a)   *Murhetta, murhetta, murhetta.*
260) <u>SAFER</u>: sor(h)row, sor(h)row,//sor(h)row?
261) <u>KNUTAS</u>: yes **loss** (.5)
     a)   *Rakastetun menetystä.*
262) of er loved ones er and~the~words~go (.3)
     a)   *Sanat kuuluvat*
263) you took my (1) brain away~
     a)   *"Veit järkeni,*
264) you actually took my **sense** away (.)
     a)   *veit mieleni."*
265)   made me your slave (.)
     a)   *"Teit minusta orjasit*
266) ((Cut to footage of Koriseva singing))
267)   promised me (.)
     a)   *lupasit*
268) it would be (.) good between us~
     a)   *meille hyvää."*
269) but it only lasted for a moment (.)
     a)   *Mutta se kesti hetken,*
270) and then you left me (.)
     a)   *ja sitten jätit minut."*
271) and then it's (.)
272) **woe is** me.'
     a)   *Voi minua raukkaa.*

273) ((Footage of Koriseva singing; being crowned tango queen))
274) KORISEVA: ((Singing)) Sa taikaren//kaat multa osta nää
275)   niin sielu armaan tänä yönä vangiksesi jää.
276) ((trans.))and capture the spirit of your loved one
277)   You buy these magic earrings
278) <u>SAFER</u>: ((cut to narration, over Koriseva's singing)
279) the tango singer has become (.)
   a) *Tangolaulajista on tullut*
280)   the **speak**ing surrogate (.)
281)   for the **silent** Finn. (.)
   a) *hiljaisten suomalaisten puolestapuhujia.*
282) **he** or she says things *h
   a) *Hän sanoo asioita,*
283)   that no mere **civi**lian would dare **utter** publicly (.)
   a) *joista ei puhuta julkisesti*
284)   or even privately. (1)
   a) *eikä yksityisestikään.*
285) Arya Koriseva has performed this public service
   a) *Arja Koriseva on suorittanut tätä julkista tehtävää*
286)   just about **every** night *h
   a) *lähes joka ilta*
287) since she was crowned **tango** queen of Finland in 1989.
   a) *siitä asti kun hänet kruunattiin Suomen tangokuningattareksi 1989.*
288) <u>KORISEVA</u>: ((cut to interviewing))
289) somehow I feel when I sing tango *h
   a) *Laulaessani tangoa minusta tuntuu*
290) that I'm talking with **their** lips
   a) *kuin puhuisin heidän puolestaan.*
291) They are not speaking~
   a) *He eivät puhu.*
292) They are shy *h
   a) *He ovat ujoja.*
293) but they would like to say the things I'm saying
   a) *Mutta haluaisivat ehkä sanoa asioita, joista minä laulan.*
294)   maybe. (1) (hhh)
295) ((Footage of Finns dancing the tango))
296) <u>SAFER</u>: *((cut to narration))*
297) Arya says that when she started performing (.)
   a) *Kun Arja aloitti,*
298) she was considered a *freak* by Finnish standards. (.)
   a) *häntä pidettiin Suomessa kummajaisena.*
299)   **why is that girl laughing** (.)

300) the critics asked. (1)
  a) *Kriitikot kysyivät:"Miksi hän nauraa?"(sentences 299–300)*
301) her audiences have learned to *glum*ly accept (.)
  a) *Yleisö on oppinut hyväksymään*
302) this jolly (.) and eccentric (.) chanteuse.
  a) *tämän iloisen laulajattaren.*
303) ((cut to interview with Koriseva))
304) SAFER: but are they having fun?=
  a) *Onko heillä hauskaa?*
305) KORISEVA: They do, but they d (.)
  a) *On, mutta*
306) just doesn't show it
  a) *he eivät näytä sitä.*
307) I don't know why (hhh)
  a) *En tiedä miksi.*
308) ((Footage of applause after a dance; Koriseva and Safer))
309) SAFER: But quite apart from these men you see in the *dance* floors (.)
  a) *He ovat hyvin erilaisia kun he ovat tanssilattialla.*
310) do Finnish men find it difficult to talk to you? for example? (.)
  a) *Onko suomalaisten miesten vaikea puhua esimerkiksi sinulle?*
311) KORISEVA: *h Older (.) men er will speak wi~to me *easily* (.)
  a) *Vanhemmat miehet puhuvat minulle helpommin*
312) than the younger ones. (2)
  a) *kuin nuoret*
313) Maybe that's (h)why (h)I'm (h)single
  a) *Ehkä sen takia olen yhä naimaton.*
314) *h (hhhhh) *h (hhhhhh) *hh (hhh) *h (hh)
315) ((Footage of Schultz and Safer))
316) SAFER: Do people tell? (1.5) each other that (.5)
  a) *Kertovatko ihmiset toisilleen*
317) they **love** each other?=
  a) *rakastavansa toisiaan?*
318) SCHULTZ: **NO:::** *o*h, my God **NO:** (.5) **NO** (.)
  a) *Herrajumala, ei!*
319) not even (.) I mean~even (.) lovers (.)
  a) *Tuskin edes rakastavaiset.*
320) **i think**
321) ((Footage of Safer and Knutas))
322) KNUTAS: Well, I'd say (.)
323) you could say it once in a lifetime
  a) *Ehkä sellaista sanotaan kerran elämässä.*
324) if you (.5) say, you have been married for (.)

"TANGO FINLANDIA"

      a)   *Jos on ollut naimisissa*
325)   for 20 years *h perhaps your (.)
      a)   *20 vuotta*
326)   spouse (.)
      a)   *ja puoliso*
327)   is on her deathbed
      a)   *on kuolinvuoteellaan.*
328)   you could comfort her with saying
      a)   *Silloin häntä voi lohduttaa sanomalla:*
329)   I love you //*h bute er:: (2)
      a)   *"Minä rakastan sinua."*
330) <u>SAFER</u>: (hhh)
331) <u>KNUTAS</u>: *it's not funny*
      a)   *Se ei ole hauskaa.*
332) ((Footage of Koriseva and Safer))
333) <u>KORISEVA</u>: It's easier to me to say *h
      a)   *Minun on helpompaa sanoa*
334)   like to my: boyfriend
      a)   *poikaystävälleni*
335)   that (in a sultry whisper) **I love you**
      a)   *"I love you"*
336) it's *h we have heard it on on TV on movies // (.)
      a)   *Koska olemme kuulleet sellaista elokuvissa.*
337) it's *h easier for me to say *h I love you=
      a)   *Minun on helpompaa sanoa "I love you"*
338) SAFER: (hhh)
339) KORISEVA: =than *h **minä rakastan sinua**
      a)   *kuin "minä rakastan sinua".*
340) it's (.)
341) doesn't heard very nice if I say *h
342) I love you in Finni//sh.
      a)   *Sanat eivät kuulosta niin hyviltä. (sentences 340–342)*
343) <u>SAFER</u>: You look slightly //embarrassed
      a)   *Sinua hieman hävettää*
344) when you say it in Finnish.
      a)   *sanoa se suomeksi.*
345) KORISEVA: (hhhh) *h yeah *h but we don't use (.)
      a)   *Niin. Me emme sano*
346)   I love you (.)
      a)   *sitä*
347)   so much as **you** do. (.)
      a)   *yhtä usein kuin te.*

348) you love almost (.) **almost everybody**
    a)   *Te rakastatte melkein kaikkia.*
349) (hhhhhhh) *h
350) When a Finnish guy or man says
    a)   *Kun suomalainen mies sanoo*
351)   I love you (.)
    a)   *rakastavansa,*
352) He really **means** it (.)
    a)   *hän tarkoittaa sitä.*
353) I know (hhh).
    a)   *Minä tiedän sen.*

                                              (Footage of Finnish band)
                                              (Credits)

What should we say about all of that?

Chapter 3

Cultural Discourses in "Tango Finlandia"

Some Initial Observations (with an American Accent)

Readers of the preceding chapter, as well as viewers of the original *60 Minutes* segment, will see for themselves that this televised program is at once entertaining, apparently informative, and deeply intriguing. It includes language produced by American speakers of English, as well as by Finnish speakers of English; it includes characterizations in American English of Finns and Finland; it also includes characterizations by Finnish English speakers of Finns and Americans; even though most expressions in the document are in English, throughout there are occasional statements in Finnish that are written (like street signs or the sign about selecting dance partners), sung (e.g., lines 274–275), or spoken (e.g., line 339); to these linguistic dynamics are added rich visual landscapes of people in their routine city life in Helsinki, in special festive occasions in other Finnish cities, in the countryside, and in tango halls, as well as visual images from a variety of other scenes including Finnish Lapland. Close-ups are included of various Finnish and American speakers.

The principal American speakers in the document are the *60 Minutes* correspondent, Morley Safer, and the American journalist in Helsinki, Teri Schultz. The principal Finnish speakers are the Finnish media personality, Jan Knutas; the tango singer, Arja Koriseva; and the Finnish historian of tango, Ilpo Hakasalo. In this chapter we draw attention to a few features in the discourse of this rich document which allow two views of the matters at hand to exist simultaneously. We use three concepts to understand this dynamic; one is *double vision*, another is *echoing structure*, and yet another is *parallel voices*. By describing these features in the discourse, we are presenting our basic descriptive findings, which can be characterized as follows. This document is being created, viewed, and verbalized in two deeply cultural ways, and thus we draw attention to this as a double vision; the differences escape the notice of participants who often believe they are saying the same things so we write about that in two ways as parallel voices (which do not necessarily overlap) and as a deceptive echoing structure (one that deceptively sounds like it is repeating the other). We will resist initially drawing general conclusions about these dynamics until we demonstrate more deeply how both an American and a Finnish discourse are differently involved in these matters. These discourses will take shape, and meaning, more forcefully in the following chapters where each view comes into focus more clearly.

THE DESCRIPTIVE FINDINGS IN A NUTSHELL

We observe initially here a few features in the construction of a double vision itself. We do so in the following ways. First, we draw attention to a sequential structure in this discourse—what we call an "echoing structure" in the text. We discuss how this type of discourse is being used here within a larger journalistic genre of constructing a puzzle or a problem, identifying responses to it, and then creating further attention-getting puzzles relative to the problem and its responses. We show how these discursive dynamics—of a verbal structure within the genre—are active for participants, but also how they are fundamentally different from the vantage point of each principal cultural discourse at play in and about this journalistic report. Eventually, we introduce the concept of "parallel voices" as a way of conceptualizing how the different cultural discourses are active simultaneously but are typically unrecognized by each, thus creating two verbalized views or two ways of hearing the same phenomena. We conceptualize this entire dynamic generally as a "double vision."

AN ECHOING SEQUENTIAL STRUCTURE: TALKING OVER DIVERSITY

Notice at the onset that this televised segment is designed through a rough dialogic form as a way of creating the impression that its production is a kind of collaborative or dialogic performance. Here are some of the ways this works:

316) <u>SAFER</u>: Do people tell? (1.5) each other that (.5)
    a)   *Kertovatko ihmiset toisilleen*
317) they **love** each other?=
    a)   *rakastavansa toisiaan?*
318) <u>SCHULTZ</u>: **NO:::** oh, my God **NO:** (.5) **NO** (.)
    a)   *Herrajumala, ei!*
319) not even (.) I mean~even (.) lovers (.)
    a)   *Tuskin edes rakastavaiset.*
320) ***I think***
321) ((Footage of Safer and Knutas))
322) <u>KNUTAS</u>: Well, I'd say (.)
323) you could say it once in a lifetime
    a)   *Ehkä sellaista sanotaan kerran elämässä.*

324)   if you (.5) say, you have been married for (.)
   a)   *Jos on ollut naimisissa*
325)   for 20 years *h perhaps your (.)
   a)   *20 vuotta*
326)   spouse (.)
   a)   *ja puoliso*
327)   is on her deathbed
   a)   *on kuolinvuoteellaan.*
328)   you could comfort her with saying
   a)   *Silloin häntä voi lohduttaa sanomalla:*
329)   I love you //*h bute er:: (2)
   a)   "*Minä rakastan sinua.*"
330) SAFER: (hhh)
331) KNUTAS: **it's not funny**
   a)   *Se ei ole hauskaa.*

The American journalist Morley Safer asks, "Do people tell each other that they love each other" followed by another American journalist's response (on lines 318–319) that even lovers do not say "I love you" to each other. Immediately after that the Finnish media personality Jan Knutas says (on lines 322–323), "Well, I'd say you could say it once in a lifetime."

Note the similar pattern here:

184) SAFER: there are strict **rules** to Finnish tango
   a)   *Suomalaisessa tangossa on tiukat säännöt.*
185) KNUTAS: the women stand on one side as you've seen
   a)   *Naiset seisovat toisella puolella*
186)   the men stand on the other
   a)   *ja miehet toisella*
187) SAFER ((Voiceover))
188) **the men** (.)
189) for **them** (.)
   a)   *Miehet*
190) there is an **unwritten** code of behavior.
   a)   *seuraavat kirjoittamatonta käyttäytymissääntöä.*
191) KNUTAS: ((Voiceover))
192) it's **good** (.)
   a)   *On hyvä,*
193)   if the man is *h sober enough *h
   a)   *jos mies on tarpeeksi selvin päin*
194)   to be able to *h make half of the dance steps
   a)   *jotta hän selviytyy tanssiaskelista*

195)   and *h not step on the woman's feet too much.
   a)   eikä tallo liikaa naisen varpaille
196) ((Footage of Knutas and Safer))
197) <u>KNUTAS</u>: he should not (.)
   a)   Hän ei saisi
198)   smell of vomit or anything
   a)   haista oksennukselle
199) ((Footage of Safer laughing)) (.2)
200)   and then (.)
201) he should not sort of try to
   a)   Mies ei saa
202)   impose himself on the woman.
   a)   tyrkyttää itseään.
203) he=he shouldn't make the woman feel uneasy
   a)   Naisella pitää olla turvallinen olo
204) he=he should be the perfect gentleman
   a)   Miehen on oltava täydellinen herrasmies.

The American correspondent Morley Safer says (on line 184), "there are strict rules to Finnish Tango," after which the Finnish man Jan Knutas responds with an illustration (185–186), "The women stand on one side as you've seen, the men on the other." The point is reiterated with Safer saying (on line 190), "there is an unwritten code of behavior," with Knutas then apparently repeating and elaborating the "code" (on lines 191–204), concluding that the man "should be the perfect gentleman."

This structuring of the discourse occurs through a form we call an "echoing sequential structure." The echoing effect is achieved as a speaker's comment from one cultural stance is followed by a culturally different other's. As a result, the other's subsequent comment is hearable by viewers as an apparent echo of the first speaker's comments, thereby reiterating and agreeing with it. In short, the second comment is typically heard to be repeating to some degree the content of the prior speaker's turn. This sequential form of a comment being followed by an apparent agreement, or by an apparent elaboration of the previous comment, creates an act sequence that is hearable by viewers as a shared collaborative or dialogic performance regarding the matter being discussed.

In the preceding, this produces the following specific discursive dynamics: an infrequent expression of "love" is hearable or reframed as a "once in a lifetime" experience; women standing here and men standing there is hearable or reframed as "strict rules" and an "unwritten code." A situation is collaboratively described by a speaker from one speech community followed by another speaker from another. Although the speakers may be using different ways of speaking, as members of different speech communities, the sequence comes across as one with a shared or common form and meaning. In short, we observe initially that this discourse pattern comes across as presuming and creating a shared meaning (this is the **apparent** echo), but does so via different meanings within each speech community (these are the parallel voices). Trying to see, hear, and speak both simultaneously results in a double vision. Let us illustrate in some more detail what we mean by this.

In the beginning of the document (lines 24–27), Morley Safer refers to Finns as "brooding" and "private," as "grimly in touch with no one but themselves," as the "shyest people on earth," and as "depressed and proud of it." Soon after these and other characterizations, Jan Knutas refers to Finns (lines 41–47) as "a silent, brooding people" who "think a lot." Knutas says Finns like "to keep our privacy and give the fellow man his privacy, keep a distance."

As with the previous example, the way the discourse is constructed places Knutas' comments in a place to be heard as "echoing" what Safer said earlier and its characterization of Finns. As a result, viewers may hear Knutas' comment about "brooding" to be confirming what Safer has said; for example, that Finns are "grimly in touch with no one but themselves" as well as being "depressed and proud of it."

This dynamic continues. Safer adds (on lines 51–54) that "Finns have a difficult time making even the most casual social contact with a stranger on the bus for example." Knutas apparently "echoes" this thought about social life on a bus by saying (on lines 58–71), "I might have to engage in a conversation. It's a horrifying thought . . . I would like to say please leave me alone and let me brood for an hour." Taken together, Knutas' comments can be heard to echo Safer's, creating the impression that both are saying the same thing: Finns don't want to talk; they want to be alone and "brood."

Eventually, through the same sequential form, Safer discusses a related feature of Finnish social life when he talks with the American reporter Teri Schultz (on lines 95–98). Together they, two Americans, report an espoused difficulty Finns have "shaking hands," with an even greater aversion to "hugging." Safer summarizes this range of features as "Finland's icy reserve" (on line 102), then immediately after this (on lines 104–109), the Finnish Tango singer, Arja Koriseva, is made to "echo" this through her statement: "We have like a wall here [between people who don't know each other]," we "look" and "watch" people "before we dare to . . . speak with you."

Ms. Koriseva says, we "look" before we "dare" speak. Introduced as an "icy reserve," her comment strongly implies consent to the earlier remarks of Safer and Schultz, that as cold people we certainly would not presume to touch you! Again, and apparently, a point has been collaboratively made through the dialogic form of the comment-echo: "Finns have a difficult time making social contact."

We could carry this analysis onward with more discursive details such as Safer's claims (on lines 117–118) that Finns "are terribly shy" to which Knutas replies, "we think that is the natural way to be" (on line 121). Or later, Safer characterizes themes in Finnish tango lyrics as "sadness" and "melancholy" (lines 234,

237), to which the Finnish tango expert, Hakasalo, replies (on lines 236–239), "We are very melancholy people here in Finland, and we need that." In each instance, a comment by an American speaker is made, followed by a Finnish speaker, with the Finnish speaker's comments being hearable, through this echoing structure, as confirming the earlier American comment. This echoing structure—or, more precisely, the Finnish speaker apparently echoing the American—is active throughout the document as we shall see.

We observe, then, to begin that one interactional dynamic through which this document is produced is prominently, but not exclusively, a play on a dialogic, collaborative sequence, through which a comment from one cultural stance is followed by another comment from a different cultural stance, but given the sequence, the latter is hearable as a confirmation of the former, at least from the vantage of the former speaker—as well as those who share that speaker's stance. In this case, an American reporter's comment creates a frame for a subsequent Finnish speaker, a spot into which a member of the Finnish speech community steps. As a result, the latter—the non-native English speaker's comment—is easily hearable as an echo of the former. The Finnish sound is not heard but given shape and meaning within the earlier American speaker's frame.

Eventually, in our subsequent chapters, we want to demonstrate that this "echoing effect"—real for viewers but only apparent upon close inspection—can create considerable misunderstandings and confusion. How? The echo is hearable as such only within the confines and the presumptions of one of the cultural discourses at play in the document—as illustrated here through an "American discourse"—without noticing that there are actually—in this case—two nonechoing sounds. Interpreted another way, there is not an echo here, but a contra-voicing of the matters at hand. There is not one but two cultural discourses being expressed about the matter, in a parallel way. The echoing structure of the discourse, therefore, is an illusion as some listeners presume speakers are saying the same thing within one cultural discourse, rather than saying different things through two cultural discourses. The echo one hears, then, is caught within the walls of one's own cultural canyon, as one can easily miss the voice of difference altogether, coming from elsewhere, from the rim above or beyond one's own cultural walls. We explore these discourses and dynamics in detail in what follows.

A FORM OF PROBLEM-RESPONSE-PUZZLE: A JOURNALISTIC FORM IS CULTIVATING ASTONISHMENT

We want to observe a second larger discursive form, perhaps one culture of reporting, a consensus narrative (Campbell, 1991), which organizes this document generally. The document proceeds through a form that could be characterized broadly, especially for American viewers, or other non-Finnish viewers, as a problem-response-puzzle form.

The first part of the broadcast (lines 1–126) sets up a *puzzle or problem* for the viewer. The visual and verbal portrait casts Finns as a people who are "isolated," "suffer the permanent glooms," "brooding," "shy," who want not to be noticed, are "private," don't seek social contact with others, "glory in their isolation," and speak a language impenetrable to outsiders (i.e., an "alphabet soup gone crazy"). Safer summarizes all of this (on lines 128–129) as a "clinical shyness," an "almost terminal melancholy." The viewer is faced with a difficult puzzle or problem of understanding a people who are so characterized. The circumstances are problematized as Safer asks, "So what do they do about this?". If one wondered whether any of this was indeed a problem to Finns, the thought is quickly abandoned, for the presumptions in Safer's question itself seem to make it so. If people are so depressed-shy-brooding, then these are certainly problems, and something—the American viewer easily presumes—should be done about them!

The second part of the segment provides a *response* to these apparent problems. How do Finns deal with being shy, brooding, private, and sad? In short, they "tango"! The tango dance is shown as people dance in the streets, in the forests, and during summer festivals, with some footage showing couples dancing the tango even on roadsides and in "the deep deep woods" (line 154). The point is summarized: Finnish tango is "everywhere" (line 149). Through it, distance between people is bridged; there is a "license to touch" (line 168) as well as clear rules—apparently needed to address Finnish anxiety—for social contact (as both Schultz describes on lines 172–181 and Knutas describes on lines 197–204).

But, this Finnish tango "is not to be confused with the groin-grinding, passionate, Latin American version" (lines 211–212). If not that, then what is it? It is, according to Safer, a "sad shuffle in a minor key" (lines 214–215) which reaffirms a Finnish "couple's instinctive sense of hopelessness" (lines 216–217). Finnish tango specialist, Hakasalo echoes this point by saying that tango lyrics are "melancholy stories . . . and we need that" (lines 221, 239). These are "love songs," yes, but "love that is over," or love for which one waits for twenty years, or love that one is sure "never will come" (lines 246–250). As a result, the songs involve "sorrow, sorrow, sorrow" (lines 259–260) and "loss" (lines 261–272).

While the tango songs highlight love stories of sadness, melancholy, and pessimism, this point is followed by another. In the end, "love" is not typically, nor should it be frequently, expressed verbally between lovers. Schultz's adamant exclamation that lovers in Finland do not exchange "I love you" (line 318) is followed by Knutas' echo that lovers might say such a thing "once in a lifetime" (line 323). Morley Safer laughs (line 330), but Knutas intervenes with a parallel cultural voice unlike Safer's laugh saying, "It's not funny" (line 331).

In concluding, then, Arja Koriseva continues similarly; she makes the point that she can say "I love you" in English more easily than she can say "minä rakastan sinua," the Finnish "equivalent." Her point, among others, is that Finnish speakers find the English words lighter and more easily usable than the Finnish ones. The Finnish version is more potent and thus used less frequently, for it carries more force and relatively deeper meanings. As the vivacious songstress says rather playfully at the conclusion of the document, unlike Finns, American speakers seem to say "I love you" to "almost everybody" (line 348). Her tone turns more serious as she concludes, "When a Finnish guy or man says I love you, he really means it, I know" (lines 350–353).

The final parts of the document leave the viewer, at least many American viewers, trapped in a *puzzle*. The tango solves problems by offering a cultural scene for touching, a means of social contact, and comfortable gendered routines. But it does so through emotional themes of sadness and melancholy that are deemed "necessary." And these are being emphasized while verbal expressions of "love" are dis-preferred and nearly nonexistent. These issues, then, leave the viewer in a discursive maze, cycling back through the document of shy, sad, tango-ing Finns, wondering what they have just seen and heard.

PARALLEL VOICES: OPENING DOORS TO TWO CULTURAL DISCOURSES

We have found it instructive at times in our analyses to separate the comments in the document that were being made by the speakers of American English from those that were made by speakers of Finnish English. In other words, what happens when we listen to this document outside of its "echoing sequential structure" and outside of its "problem-response-puzzle" form?

We will focus on this type of analysis in the next several chapters. For now, let us look briefly at the American speakers' comments alone, then at the Finnish speakers'. We do so in order to introduce two communication codes that are hearable in the document as two distinctly parallel cultural discourses, both of which we develop in our subsequent analyses.

An American Voice

To begin, notice in the American English speakers' language and social interaction several things. As we noted earlier, Morley Safer's language characterizes Finns as "brooding, private, grimly in touch with no one but themselves, the shyest people on earth, depressed and proud of it" (lines 24–27). Similarly, his language depicts Finns as having "a difficult time making even the most casual social contact with a stranger on the bus for example" (lines 51–54). Finns are diagnosed as "terribly shy" (line 117), clinically shy (line 128), and fraught with "terminal melancholy" (line 129). These are his statements formulated through his popular American English. The other American in the segment, Teri Schultz, describes "very strict parameters of Finnish social being" (lines 173–174), a fear of being "overtly sexy" (line 179), and an aversion to saying "I love you" (lines 318–320).

We repeat these examples of this language as reminders of the American English being used in the segment and its way of characterizing Finnish people and practices. Treating these linguistic expressions on their own, for their own sake, draws attention to a cultural stance that is active within this document. It is a voice that is used to produce and interpret the televised text as a whole, including the Finnish images accompanying it. We are tempted to refer to it as a cultural black hole which sucks into it anything nearby! Drawing attention to this now is useful in another way. It points out a contrast between this discourse in American English and a parallel Finnish cultural discourse, which is also active in the text, and in Finnish viewers' comments about it. So, there is not just an American galactic discourse at play, but another. Let's introduce this other discourse now, on its own, for its own sake.

A Finnish Voice

We can focus our initial observations of this Finnish discourse by asking: What kind of communication is Mr. Knutas, Ms. Koriseva, and Hakasalo producing here? We could notice each is reporting, at least in part, about their culture to an outsider, or to one who is unfamiliar with Finland. Their verbal accounts, as a result, portray something about Finnish culture in this intercultural context to the American, Mr. Safer. For example, Mr. Knutas discusses Finns as "silent, brooding people who think a lot" (lines 41–42). Ms. Koriseva discusses how "a wall" is presumed between people for purposes of respect and privacy (lines 104–109). Hakasalo says we Finns "need" that "melancholy" feature which is not "totally pessimistic" (on lines 221 and following). We could further characterize each as a kind of cultural account or an explanation of Finnish culture being constructed for an outsider.

In the case of Ms. Koriseva, she gives cultural reasons for what Safer has called in the broadcast a Finns' "difficulty making social contact," or in American English a Finnish "icy reserve." She puts it differently; Finns conduct initial and important social affairs in a properly observant way, from behind a "wall." From there, one monitors whether "joining others" is intrusive or might be done appropriately. To assess the scene, one carefully watches others and deciphers the social scene before "daring" to speak to another, especially someone one does not know well. In this sense, Koriseva wants Safer to know that cultural preparation needs to occur, even if in a split second, prior to an act of "speaking with another." One should not just assume talking with someone is good social manners! She also wants Safer to know that "speaking with another" is not presumably what should be done with ease, but something that might be done, and if so, it should be done with the proper preparatory care and caution. Her report emphasizes a kind of

Table 3-1 Key Terms and Symbolic Clusters in the Two Cultural Discourses

Key Term	Finnish Symbolic Cluster	US English Symbolic Cluster
Brooding	Silent, thoughtful, private, distant	Grim, shy, depressed
Social Stance	A wall between; watch and look carefully before speaking with another	Difficult time making social contact, icy reserve
Shyness	A natural way to be; not to stick out	Terribly, clinically shy
Sadness	We are melancholy and we need that	Why this sadness, this terminal melancholy?

considerateness, a vigilant attentiveness that should be exercised before one goes to speak with another, especially in initial and important encounters.

Note, then, that our initial observations of a Finnish discourse here are focused on an event of speaking about one's culture to an outsider generally, and we note within that event the way a cultural explanation of one's practices is being formulated for an outsider. Cultures and their discourses live in such practices—both in the reports about the practice for others and in its very enactment when with one's own (see Table 3-1).

Let us focus briefly here on the idea of "daring to speak" as it is active in Ms. Koriseva's explanation (and as one way to summarize the dynamics displayed in Table 3-1). As it turns out, this can be a very potent cultural phrase and action within a Finnish discourse. The Finnish idea brings with it several cultural premises: one should be attentive to others; one should respect the autonomy and privacy of others and not simply presume they want to be contacted socially; it is best if caution is exercised in contacting others or in verbally connecting with them; at times it is better to be silent than to engage in talk that is unnecessary or infringes upon them. These are only some of the Finnish premises active in Ms. Koriseva's conversational account. Indeed, in Finnish, these ideas are expressed in a much larger system of meaning that the word, "dare," or its Finnish version, "*uskaltaudumme*" in the transcript, or similarly "*rohjeta*," can activate.

This parallel Finnish discourse is elaborated even further. Note that Ms. Koriseva contrasts the Finnish account with another, presumably "American" one. She wants Safer to understand how the Finnish stance is explicitly unlike an American one that is freely expressive of its feelings, intents, and thoughts, for "you [Americans] love almost everybody"! A Finnish expressive system can be much more cautious about interactions with others, and about the verbal expression of emotions, especially the strong emotion of love. Speaking about it, Ms. Koriseva wants Safer to know, can and at times should be done, but rarely, as in the use of fine wine, when it is deemed fitting for some special occasion.

Cultural Discourses as Stances for Speaking and Viewing

Our comments in this chapter serve as initial observations, as orientations to several dynamics in the broadcast itself. These include a structure which is designed as an echoing of utterances but upon closer consideration is only apparently that. This sequence occurs within a larger problem-response form, in two parallel cultural voices that are active in and about this complex text itself. Note that each dynamic earlier—what is echoing what, what is problematic, and what is puzzling—can be viewed, and as we will see next is being viewed, from the distinct perspective of each of the discourses. This is the double vision we notice and work toward.

We now turn to one such discourse in more detail: the third column of the table, a popular "US discourse," which was used within it as well as to view and speak about this televised document.

Chapter 4

A Popular US American Discourse about Finns as Others

In this chapter, we explore the nature of the reports produced by viewers in the United States immediately after watching the *60 Minutes* episode of "Tango Finlandia." This discourse, as a whole, is composed of several parts. In particular, these cultural reports focus upon the topics of Finland and Finns; expressed astonishment at Finns and Finland; rendered Finns as inexpressive, sad, and shy; diagnosed this portrayal as a problem; and offered some remedies for this problem. Hidden in this discourse is the way making sense of a cultural other actually reflects more about one's own cultural frame of reference, one's own coding, one's own "majority culture" as Professor Thorburn of MIT has put it, rather than it reveals something about the cultural other. Let's listen to what was said by these viewers in some more detail.[1]

FIRST IMPRESSIONS OF "TANGO FINLANDIA": A DISCURSIVE THEME OF ASTONISHMENT

Upon viewing this episode, a 23-year-old female from Massachusetts said: "I'm baffled at how a whole society could live like that." A 21-year-old female from New York said: "I can't fathom living in a world without love." A 25-year-old female noticed that Finns have "a way of interacting, and a view of relationships which is drastically different from those we're familiar with in the US. 'Depth' seems valued over 'maintenance' of relationships." Just as Safer puzzled over what he called, a "national mission . . . to not be noticed" (lines 9–10) and Schultz couldn't understand why "nobody would want to talk to me" in Finland (line 86), these remarks expressed considerable puzzlement about this place called Finland and its people.

A general first impression was formulated: the Finnish "society" or "world" is remarkably, even amazingly, "drastically different" from the one(s) familiar to the commentator. Several visual images were mentioned from the video as particularly forceful and memorable in formulating this amazement. US viewers described the expression on Finnish faces as "glum" or "dour" or "expressionless." In particular, they found it hard to believe that these were the faces of people freely dancing the tango, simply waiting for a bus, or walking down the streets. In fact, it would be difficult for us to overemphasize the degree to which the Finnish face was noticed initially, commented upon, and mentioned in these cultural reports (see later). The question was posed repeatedly: "Why are they so unhappy?"

Other visual images were also mentioned, such as the use of lighted signs to indicate whether the current dance provided a man or a woman the opportunity to choose a dancing partner. Mentioned also prominently were statements made by the primary Finnish speakers in the video, Knutas and Koriseva in particular, about Finns not being eager to engage in conversations. These images and these Finnish comments struck many viewers in the United States as deeply perplexing, thus producing discourses, like those earlier, that were baffled at these peculiar ways, of this nearly unfathomable world. We call this coupling of phrasing with images, a discursive theme of astonishment.

When this discourse was developed somewhat verbally, as in the previous comments, specific sites of this difference were mentioned, such as the place of "love" in the society, its unusual "way of interacting," and its unusual "view of relationships." Only very rarely was a potentially positive quality mentioned, such as the society's "depth," as a way of understanding this startled first impression of difference. One discursive theme is thus prominent in this discourse. It is composed with these words and images, involves remarks about cultural differences, and amazement that "a whole society could live like that," even if with "depth."

Typically, however, as we will see, the different world of Finland was cast in this initial discourse not positively as deep, but in a rather less favorable light.

NOT US(UAL): DISCOURSING FINNS AS INEXPRESSIVE, SAD, AND SHY

The US discourse formulated a general impression of Finns as inexpressive, sad, and shy. This was done in a variety of ways, with each combining specific words and phrases, often by reference to the Finnish faces.

The broadcast images of the Finnish face occurred in combination with other images and comments. For example, some interpreted the faces by using Safer's and Knutas' echoing of the term "brooding," and Hakasalo's "melancholy" or Safer's, Knutas', and others' terms, such as "shy" or "depressed" or "uncommunicative." Some commentators recalled Safer's phrase, with Finnish faces being shown while he said, "This is not a day of national mourning in Helsinki" (on line 21)—even though to Safer and to viewers, it apparently looked that way, as it was verbally expressed in that way. Viewers also emphasized that these facial images, when coupled with not saying the Finnish equivalent of "I love you" and the dance floor signs, were the predominant bases for the impressions of Finns as inexpressive, as sad, and as shy.

Listen, for example, to this 21-year-old female who, immediately after viewing the episode, put her initial impression about Finns and Finland this way:

> They are sad people, don't express feelings; very shy. It is a cold, dreary and lonely place.

Consider similarly, this formulation of a 21-year-old female from Boston:

> I feel Finns are unemotional, shy individuals, afraid of expressing their true personality. Why are they so depressed?

A 20-year-old female from Massachusetts said a bit more, echoing especially Safer, Knutas, and Hakasalo:

> They are reticent, brooding, melancholy (and like it), don't make eye contact or are not comfortable touching, talking or being with other people. They need music and a light telling them what to do in order to socialize.

Three general clusters of terms come together in this discursive construction of Finns. One includes terms and phrases like, "don't express feelings," "afraid of expressing their true personality," "reticent," "don't make eye contact," "not comfortable touching," "inexpressive" and the like. We entitle this cluster as "**inexpressive.**" A second includes terms and phrases like "very shy," "shy individuals," "reticent," not "comfortable being with other people," need help socializing, and the like. We entitle this cluster as "**shy.**" A third cluster of terms includes "sad," "dreary," "depressed," "melancholy," and the like. We entitle this cluster, "**sad.**" Taken together, then, these are basic terms that accompany the viewers' recounting of focal images of faces, dance signs, and not saying "I love you." Together, these create a first impression of Finns and Finland as inexpressive, shy, and sad. We emphasize that the negative image created surprised us, for we had asked viewers only for first impressions, not for negative impressions!

Privacy

We do want to note briefly one additional term that was used by viewers in the United States. After closer inspection, we found one potentially neutral to positive cluster of descriptors in the US viewer's discourse about Finland. It includes viewers' impressions of Finns as "very private" people. As a 22-year-old male succinctly put it, "They are obviously very private people." However, just as a commentator may be heard to neutrally describe, or even compliment, Finns on their

A POPULAR US AMERICAN DISCOURSE

"privacy," any positive sense of this phrase was typically taken away with the other clusters mentioned earlier. For example, a 27-year-old male from Massachusetts says,

> They're shy and don't like to express emotions. They like privacy. They don't want to stand out. They are awkward in social situations. They don't seem very happy.

Let us provide a more elaborate reading of these main discursive themes that viewers used to characterize Finns in these ways.

Inexpressive

Our corpus includes far more commentary on the "inexpressiveness" of Finns than the others. In other words, the US viewers' discourse of first impressions carries a prominent and elaborate theme, a declaration that Finns are inexpressive. In many cases, first impressions were formulated only through the terms of this cluster. Consider these few illustrative data. First, from a 20-year-old female from New York:

> They are very cold, emotionless people. They seem to be very closed off to the people around them. It is not accepted to show how you feel and must be very hard to communicate.

A 20-year-old female from Massachusetts put her similar impression in these words:

> They are very quiet and inward people. They don't seem to express themselves, or want to. They seem to be content with their selves and their lives. There is no effort to try and "be your own self," they all seem to be alike. There is no desire to be "one of a kind," they do not want to draw attention to themselves

A 22-year-old female from Massachusetts made a similar statement:

> Finns do not seem to be confident in being openly expressive about their feelings. Even when they are happy (like doing the Tango) they do not smile or express any contentment with their face. It seems very "cold" in that people are so unwilling to let you "inside."

When we asked what visual images the episode left in their mind as bases for this "inexpressiveness," viewers mentioned the following: "people weren't looking at each other," "no eye contact," "no smiles," "no facial expressions," "scared to talk on the bus or on the street." Faced with these images of Finnish faces, influenced by the televised words that declared Finns don't want to communicate with strangers or express the emotion of love, and confronted with a different world unlike their own, these viewers formulated this first impression. It elaborates, in their words, a style that is "very closed off," finds it "hard to communicate," is "very quiet and inward," and not "openly expressive." Finns are sometimes portrayed further as "cold" and "unwilling to let you 'inside.'"

Some viewers noted that this kind of inexpressiveness might sound somewhat familiar to them. In other words, some of these initial impressions were formulated with a reference to a practice that its formulator seemed to recognize and with which they could somehow identify. A 20-year-old female from California who had lived in New England for a while saw some relationship between social practices in the Northeastern part of the United States and the Finnish ones she had just observed. She constructed that link in this way:

> This reminds me of some people from New England, but even more extreme. They aren't friendly to strangers or even to each other. They are extremely private people who isolate themselves from others. I don't doubt that they have the highest suicide rate and lowest birth rate.

This response, of course, comes in the form of a judgment, from a Californian about Finnish and New England unfriendliness, which implies something better about "Californian friendliness." But she is not the only one to draw such a link. Here's a New Englander, a 23-year-old male from Boston, who somewhat concurs:

> The Finns are a lot like Bostonians in that they both find it hard to express their feelings. Finnish people might be a bit more extreme when it comes to this in that they never say "I love you," yet, Bostonians are also very cold and unfriendly and people usually do not go out of their way to say "hi."

These formulations carry a rather dubious familiarity: Finns are like those cold and unfriendly New Englanders who can't express themselves either! In other words, a regional stereotype from the United States is used to make sense of those from another nation, applying one familiar stereotype to a national other (see Petkova and Lehtonen, 2005).

As is evident here, this discourse of first impressions can carry rather strong and negative evaluations. A negative evaluation was by far the most prevalent. We searched long and hard to find something to counter this, wondering if any US viewer might see and say something else or something positive other than this.

There were a very few, more neutral impressions of inexpressiveness in our corpus. Here's one formulated by a 23-year-old male from Idaho:

> They seem reserved and shy, they seem to have well-defined ideas about what's appropriate and what's not. I wouldn't say that they seem unhappy, but that they don't seem to be very expressive or very willing to show emotion.

Rather than describing this style as cold, unfriendly, or uncaring, as earlier, this formulation is mainly descriptive, without the negative evaluation, emphasizing an appropriate way of being reserved and shy. From this viewer's comment, one need not be verbally or facially exuberant or show emotions to be doing something worthy and good.

In summary, then, the discourse of first impressions included a reaction of astonishment, with this being linked primarily to its most pronounced and elaborated theme, the so-called inexpressiveness of Finns. This theme focused on the visual images of Finnish faces in public and on buses, as it also followed on-air descriptions of these images as indexes of "mourning," "depression," and "shyness." Further, Finns were described on air and in this initial viewers' discourse as not wanting or unable to talk. These features of the discourse, this configuration of images and verbal descriptors, were framed prominently as "inexpressive" and further evaluated as closed, inward, and even cold. Although this quality was claimed at times as familiar to some in the United States, even typical in some places in the United States, it was more typically evaluated as negative. Rarely, a neutral or positive portrayal appeared. With it, Finns were described from this latter view as appropriately reserved and shy.

Sad

A theme of sadness was present in US discourse but much less frequently elaborated than the theme of inexpressiveness. The particular visual scenes that were active with this theme were, in the words of our viewers, "facial cues (no smiles, laughs),""unhappy faces in the streets,""no talking on the bus,""couldn't say 'I love you,'" and "singing unhappy songs." Viewers also mentioned the words Safer used when he described Finns as "depressed and proud of it," and when he mentioned "the high suicide rate," and "the low birth rate." These visual images were the ones most active when viewers portrayed Finland and Finns as sad. Consider these formulations.

A 34-year-old female from Massachusetts said:

> They are a very glum and melancholy bunch! There is no fun in their lives and there is nothing to look forward to, they just keep to themselves as individuals.

A 21-year-old, Italian American female said:

> They are extremely dry and unemotional people. They seem very depressed. The entire country seems depressed and unable to interact personally and socially.

A 21-year-old male from Massachusetts:

> It seems like a morbid place to live or (especially) to visit. I was reminded of a nursing home, there were few smiles, everyone moved slow, and people seemed sad.

Occasionally a comment from a viewer wrestled with this sadness as something perhaps only apparent. Might it be, in this type of formulation, that Finns express their happiness in some other way? A 20-year-old female from Massachusetts wondered:

> Finns are obviously a very melancholy people. Whether their lives are devoid of happiness or whether they just express joy and love in a different way, I couldn't tell.

Just these few comments illustrate the wide range of visual images, words, and phrases used to say something we entitle here as sadness. These comments reference visual images of faces, bus scenes, and sad songs; cast these verbally as "a very glum and melancholy bunch," which has "no fun," and "nothing to look forward to"; an "extremely dry and unemotional people," who are "very depressed"; and "a morbid place" with "few smiles" where "people seemed sad," "very melancholy," maybe even "devoid of happiness." This cluster of visual images, terms, and phrases creates a discursive theme in which Finns and Finland are portrayed as sad.

Shy

In the discourse under examination here, a third theme of shyness is also active. Earlier, viewers comment repeatedly about Finns as being "shy," "very shy," "shy individuals," or with expressions like "withdrawn," "reserved," people who "like to stay to themselves." When asked what features in the episode cued this shyness, they mentioned how "they won't look at people" (this referring also to a visual scene where a direct meeting of the eyes leads to a quick aversion of the gazes). These comments echo Safer, who said, after the image is displayed, that "no one looks anyone in the eye" (line 28). Similarly, viewers mentioned "a lack of eye contact," they "don't look anyone in the eye," or seem "withdrawn." In other words, the discursive theme of shyness carries with it a limited range of terms and phrases, and a limited range of visual images, relative to the themes of inexpressiveness and sadness.

The three main themes in this discourse formulate a report about Finns and Finland as inexpressive, sad, and shy. A minor and rarer subtheme identifies parts of the inexpressiveness and shyness as perhaps resulting from a concern for privacy. Each discursive theme brings with it, our viewers said, certain focal images and terms. All of these are configured together in a particular way to form this US discourse about this astonishing place, with its Finnish faces (while dancing the tango, walking down the street, and on buses), "the dance signs," and its infrequent use of "I love you." Together, these elements create a US discourse, produced right after viewing the television episode on *60 Minutes*, about Finns and Finland.

SOME HIDDEN WORKINGS OF THIS CULTURAL DISCOURSE

We want at this point to step outside this popular US discourse in order to introduce several observations about it, about this particular combination of visual images and their verbal framing, both within and about the document. We want to begin thinking about some of the limited ways this cultural discourse indeed works.

First, notice how this discourse is being formulated about two main topics: Finns and Finland. In other words, US viewers are formulating what they have to say by focusing on these matters, with comments about each presumably saying something about Finns, Finnishness, and Finland. This is predominantly what they report the document is about, explicitly.

Second, it is essential to understand that this discourse is deeply implicating its own cultural stance, a so-called model of US Americanness, as a taken-for-granted basis for its use, as it purportedly discusses this other, Finns and Finnishness. Note as Finns are viewed and discussed as inexpressive, sad, and shy, that this image implicates a US view of itself as quite different—in fact quite the opposite—as outgoing, happy, and extroverted. In a nutshell, then, this discourse is unknowingly rendering a cultural other through an image that contrasts with its self, and in the process the contrasting image—of the Finn—is precisely counter to its presumed cultural self. The astonished sense that these other people are not like us at all is created by noticing contrasts and then verbally casting them as negating values which are presumed in the US viewers' discourse. In the process, Finns and Finland are being filtered through this US discourse. The filtering process creates an image of Finns that opposes them to US in precisely US ways. The resulting portrayal, visually and verbally, is of an unUSual other, the inexpressive, shy, and sad Finn casting a negative shadow over the more USual one who is presumably outgoing, happy, and extroverted.[2] Although the discourse purports to be about others, it formulates others largely as a contrast to its self, and thus is caught in the terms, images, and judgments of one's cultural model.

We can summarize this discursive process as *a complex communicative dynamic of othering in which the other is cast as a negation of self through the words and images which contrast other with one's presumed self.* This is a process wherein "the other" is seen as, and said to be an inverted and differentiated version of one's cultural self, and thus casts the other in terms that contrast with its self, with all of this occurring within the un-noticed discursive web of one's own discourse. This unrecognized, implicit process is accompanied by a strong belief in the discourse by its users; while its propositional content is about a culturally different other, and purportedly crosses cultural worlds, its form of assertion remains housed in its own cultural frame. In short, this implicit cultural report of othering is only apparently about an other because its bases of judgment never leave their cultural home. The strong expression of difference and deficiency it creates about the cultural other, *as an other*, are couched within a reasserted discourse of one's own. (We develop this point in the next two chapters.)

Third, we want to emphasize, as we have indicated throughout here and in Chapter 3, that the discourse produced by US viewers echoes—and not just apparently—parts of the discourse produced in the televised episode itself. Note the analogous character of this dynamic to what we discuss in Chapter 3 as an *"echoing sequential structure."* The echoing process operates both in the original document (as discussed in Chapter 3) and in discussions about the document (as discussed here). In both, *users select images and terms about another which contrast with their own cultural discourse, using them to do the work of their own common culture, which also does the work of negating a cultural other.* Morley Safer, for example, introduces Finland as peripheral (lines 8, 37) and Finns as those who want "to not be noticed" (line 10); they are deemed "private" (lines 24, 29), and not only the "shyest people on earth" (line 26), but people who "want to be alone" (line 36). Similarly, he discusses Finland as "dark" (line 13), "suffering" (line 14), "gloomy" (line 15), in "mourning" (line 21), "grim" (line 25), and "depressed and proud of it" (line 27). As a result, his language and the visual images accompanying them portray Finland as peripheral, not talkative, shy, and depressed. Deeply implicated in this is Safer's verbal and visual discourse, its sense of centrality, extroversion, and happiness so presumably prominent in US impressions of itself. A close-up of Safer's face—at line 29—on a Helsinki street shows parts of this contrast visually. In this way, as in the earlier portrayals, Safer and viewers formulate a US discourse about Finland that employs a negating contrast (i.e., their being unlike us) and an inversion of US themes (they value what we are not). Of course, this is a discourse that is at home in the United States, but not the same in Finland, which we shall see shortly.

Finally, we notice how this discourse activates a fairly limited semantic field, or range of meanings. The US discourse being used here works within a small set of oppositions between how US viewers show and see others and what that implicates about their sense of who they are. To here, those main oppositions are, relative to Finnish and US American themes, inexpressive-outgoing, sad-happy, and shy-extroverted, with lesser ones being private-public and peripheral-central. This US cultural discourse about others thus operates largely within a rather limited semantic field, rendering a cultural other in terms and images that are not of the others' world and do not penetrate that world, but reside within a limited part of the United States' own.

DIAGNOSTIC DISCOURSE: FINNISHNESS AS PROBLEMATIC AND ITS REMEDY

As we are seeing, cultural discourses, as this US discourse, carry with them communal beliefs and values. That which is deemed factual within its terms and propositions is believed and familiar. However, when the factual or familiar is somehow negated, as when people do things counter to the ways one thinks they should be done, boundaries of coherence are stretched, and a puzzle or problem is sensed. The discourse then works to create the questions: How could they be like that, or do things like that? One might even feel it is counter to human nature to act in that way. Explanations are sought for the apparent anomaly one has seen, with colloquial accounts being given for this puzzling way of life. In short, what one sees as a contrast, something weird or a problem, needs to be explained; perhaps a diagnosis can be made, and, if so, eventually, treatment can be offered. If a people are inexpressive, sad, and shy, so the cultural logic goes, there must be a problem! Why are "they" like "that"? What is the reason or cause of that problem? Can it be helped? One type of viewer response was formulated along these lines.

Consider what this 21-year-old female from Boston had to say upon viewing "Tango Finlandia":

> My impression of Finland and Finns is of a tight, cold society. The weather definitely contributes to the shyness and lack of expression of the people. Finland seems like a rigid place and people seem devoid of warmth or emotion.

Or, similarly, from a 21-year-old female:

> Finns seem content being unhappy and alone. Maybe it is a result of the cold temperature and lack of sun. A friend of mine told me that in Seattle, Washington, people are very depressed and there is a high suicide rate. There is also very little sun in Seattle. Maybe there is a connection.

In both cases, Finland and Finns were presented through the themes of a US discourse, emphasizing their alleged "lack of expression," unhappiness, and shyness. This is coupled with a sense of problematicity, for those people are "devoid of warmth or emotion," part of a "tight, cold society," and all "alone." How can this be? Diagnostic explanations are offered: It must be the weather, the cold temperature, and the lack of sun. Maybe this is a sad nation with seasonal affective disorder? In a colder climate, with low temperatures and little sunshine, what else would be produced but cold, depressed people?

Since, it is assumed, no one would want to be inexpressive, sad, and shy—for don't we all want to be communicative, happy, and outgoing?—something should be done. In terms of this diagnosis, as the cultural logic goes further, then some treatment must be warranted. Some discourse was produced along these lines. Here are some potential remedies viewers mentioned for these alleged Finnish national maladies. A 22-year-old female from California put her formulation into these words:

> I think that it is extremely sad that they live that way and I really do not understand how anyone could be happy there—obviously they aren't. Life is all about human interaction and sharing feelings with one another—since everyone needs love and affection that is what the Finns need to start giving to each other.

From the other coast, a 22-year-old female from Massachusetts explained the situation similarly:

> I get the impression that they have not experienced life. Communication seems to be such an important part of living, yet they remain silent. They don't meet new people because they don't interact. Showing love to the ones I love makes my life whole. They show no love and never say "I love you." This could contribute to their constant state of melancholy.

What is deemed problematic in viewers' discourse is the negation of a common US discursive field. From its point of view, "they remain silent," "don't interact," and "obviously" aren't "happy." What they need, from this view, is a typical US American solution. They need to "communicate," "share their feelings with one another," show some "love and affection." If they would do this, so the cultural script goes, they could become more whole (in effect, more like US). The cultural logic could be paraphrased: if Finns would just communicate and share their feelings, they could meet new people and feel a whole lot better about themselves! That this is a prominent American (and British) discourse exercised in prominent media events has been pointed out in great detail before (Cameron, 2000; Carbaugh, 1989; Katriel and Philipsen, 1981). In this case, however, the plea is not just for "individuals" to solve their problems by communicating, but for a national culture to be changed, to solve its "problems," by "communicating." Crucial to point out here is this: the sense that there is a "problem," that it consists of "inexpressive," "sad," and "shy" people, and that it can be solved by "sharing feelings," all is being conceived and evaluated, with alleged remedies within a US discourse.

This discourse of first impressions has a kind of self-sealing quality, and as a result creates only an illusion of crossing between cultures. It is perhaps more accurate to envision this process as a kind of tragic, narcissistic cultural play. Television is providing here, through "Tango Finlandia," not a window into another cultural world, but a mirror reflecting one's own, a bit inverted, perhaps through negative images, but still showing more about one's own world than the others.

A BRIDGE TO A FINNISH DISCOURSE VIA A SHIFT IN KEY: FROM A NEWS DOCUMENT TO NATIONAL HUMOR

When US viewers wondered about the status of the show, they repeatedly reminded each other that "Tango Finlandia" did, after all, appear on the "news" program, *60 Minutes*. "This is a news program," they would say. As a result, the materials presented were watched and discussed as something akin to the evening news, a documenting of facts about and life in another country. There were, however, over the past decades, two viewers in the United States who wondered somewhat about the seriousness of this segment. Each was not entirely convinced that the episode, or maybe it was just the Finns in it, were entirely on the up-and-up. Are they really speaking the truth here? As a 21-year-old male from Boston put it:

> This is a very sad and introverted culture. Possibly the least vibrant or vital of any I've ever seen but I suspect there is a certain humor about this among some Finns, an extremely dry humor that makes British humor seem like Jerry Lewis. I like Finland!

Although he had never been to Finland, this viewer went on to say he trusts more what he sees in visual images than what he hears in the verbal statements. Perhaps he noticed a twinkle in an eye that indicated something funny was going on. A 21-year-old female from Massachusetts observed similarly.

> The reporter portrayed the Finns as cold, brooding, melancholy, silent, shy—but with many repressed feelings—they also seemed like they had a very dry sense of humor about their attitudes and lives.

These two viewers, and we emphasize only these two over the past two decades, suggest the possibility that this US discourse has taken the video all too seriously. Might some of the Finns in the video be kidding? Have they "pulled one over" on the US American correspondent and journalist? Could the US viewers have missed that some of this or some part of this was, in fact, a joke?

NOTES

1 For details of our methodology, please see the appendix.
2 The idea being introduced here of a Finnish "shadow" introduces a feature that we discuss later as a "contrastive discourse and cultural inversions." The dynamic involves a focus in this discourse on a verbal image of another that counters one's own cultural premises about being and acting. What is filtered "out" in the process is precisely the Finnish terms and meanings of its self, which we explore in subsequent chapters.

Chapter 5

A Popular Finnish Discourse
First Impressions

News of the broadcast of "Tango Finlandia" in the United States spread quickly around Finland. When first shown in the United States on February 3, 1993, the first author was in Finland doing field work. While he heard about the broadcast immediately via e-mail from friends and family in the United States, he also heard about the US broadcast from friends and colleagues in Finland within hours. Common knowledge in Finland is that Finns care deeply, perhaps too deeply, about what others think of them (Sajavaara and Lehtonen, 1997). Thus, a broadcast of this kind was bound to touch a Finnish cultural nerve. What we explore here are some of those nerves being exposed by this episode of *60 Minutes*. What we find, eventually, is not so much that this television text created a national discussion, but that the televised report was given a particular Finnish shape and meaning through a Finnish discourse, quite unlike the one we heard in the previous chapters. In particular, we find that the Finnish discourse about first impressions includes a complex set of emotions, at times a sequence of emotions. The discourse also, for some, frames the televisual text as a unique form of Finnish satire, which is both funny and serious, and is ambivalent about this form of humor, especially when used with foreigners, with the emotions and the satire saying much to Finns about Finnishness and their relations with others.

A COMPLEX SET OF FINNISH EMOTIONS: SHOULD WE LAUGH OR CRY?

While viewing the "Tango Finlandia" episode, we watched Finnish viewers laugh, sometimes very loudly. Also, we noticed as the video went along, for many, there was a mounting sense of moving from humor to irritation to aggravation and anger. These reactions were concisely summarized in short statements. One Finnish viewer, who emphasized the emotion words, said: "It was kind of *funny* and in another way it made me *angry*." Similarly, another said, "It made me angry, it made me laugh." Or simply, as a third put it, "I'm not sure if I should laugh or cry." The acute ambivalence aroused by the episode was apparent in these typical prominent first comments: from laughter to anger.

We noticed in initial discussions with Finnish viewers that right after seeing the video, there was a propensity to discuss the anger first, sometimes in a rather prolonged way. The source of the anger was generally twofold. Some were angry that Finnish participants in the video, even if humorous to Finns, were apparently colluding with foreigners and saying bad things about Finns. Although irritating and aggravating, after a while, this anger and irritation subsided. Others were angry at the American production team for putting Finns in a rather unfavorable light. This anger tended to endure longer. By the end of the video, both sources of anger tended to overshadow the reactions to earlier scenes in the video of humor. By the end, for Finnish viewers, the lighthearted atmosphere often had been replaced by irritation and/or anger, with this being the first subject of discussion. After discussing this, Finnish viewers would return to the humor in the televisual text, with the discourse embracing a complex set of emotions about and features within the document, from laughter to anger.

We wish to emphasize that some Finnish viewers found it very difficult to see any humor in the video. For example, one Finnish member of our research team was very frustrated and angry after viewing the clip for the first time. Her husband, also a member of the research team, watched the anger carry over a period of three days before finally giving way. After a few days, she decided to show the video for the first time to a group of her students. Her considerable frustration was aroused again. A male student in her class from Rauma noticed her frustration and politely mentioned: "I think this is dark humor." At that point, the lecturer "stopped in her tracks" and realized, "yes, that's what it is." This process of anger (at an "American news" report) had prevented her from hearing this video as humor (as a Finnish cultural document). This was quite common among some viewers, especially some female Finnish viewers. Also, the process of males initiating a cultural framing of this text as "dark, black humor," followed by female acknowledgment of this was quite common. Although most viewers expressed humor and irritation at the text, these came in different degrees, with all Finnish viewers eventually able to acknowledge and understand this range of emotions.

Anger and laughter were most prominently expressed; however, the range of emotions activated by the episode sometimes was broadened. For example, one viewer expressed embarrassment, saying, "THIS is not me and I don't want people to think of me this way." Another viewer elaborated on this:

> I'm ashamed of my country and I feel stupid and humiliated . . . On the other hand, I just laughed very much too, when I watched that, because it all seems so ridiculous and uncomprehensible and I get the feeling that this just can't be true . . . but it is.

In these cases, the viewers felt the video clip cast Finns and Finland in a very unfavorable and complicated light that was both funny and not. As a result, the emotions aroused were rather clear, on the surface, from laughter to anger, yet the reasons for them were complicated and ran much more deeply. This is something the Finnish discourse will make clear, which was missed within the televised episode, with this—the missing of the prominent Finnish cues—being another cause for anger, or embarrassment, or humiliation. In this sense, and upon deeper Finnish reflection, the video was hardly a laughing matter.

The Finnish discourse shows us how it is possible to hear these emotions as keyed to specific parts of the video clip. As a result, the emotions are discussed as active in different ways at different times in the televised episode. Consider, as examples, the following verbal interpretations, formulated as emotions being keyed to particular moments in the episode and whether statements were being made by American or Finnish participants:

> In the beginning Finland was introduced in a nasty way to Americans, for example, by telling about our suicide rates and our expressions on the buses! That wasn't funny at all, even if it was meant to be. The funny part came when Finnish people started to talk about Finns. They knew what to say and how to say it to be able to make a point *and* make it sound funny.

According to this viewer, what "wasn't funny at all" was the American Safer's mentioning of suicide rates along with the visual footage, mainly of people's faces on public streets, on the buses. This, it appears to this viewer, was an outsider making fun of Finns and went beyond what was humorous. This is troublesome and even more irritating to some Finns, for some of the Finnish faces shown were labeled "unattractive," even "pathetic." While these visual scenes and Safer's editorial comments were not considered humorous, funny scenes did appear elsewhere, especially as the Finnish commentators in the video spoke about Finland and the United States.

One Finnish viewer's discourse linked emotions in a sequence to particular scenes in the episode and to the American correspondent from earlier to later scenes:

> First it made me laugh, really. The American reporter had found all sad and desperate people in the streets. But about in the middle of the program I started to feel a bit annoyed, 'cause the American didn't find any good things, even if they exist.

Here, we find the "first" laughter refers to the early part of the video where the footage of people on the streets is shown, along with comments by Finnish participants. This precipitated much laughter from Finnish viewers. As the camera pans across people waiting for a bus, an image this viewer calls "sad and desperate people in the streets," this strikes some Finnish viewers as funny. The exaggerated scenes of tango dancing also created laughter for many viewers. However, later, "about in the middle of the program," the humor subsides. Although we cannot be exactly sure at what point this happened for this one viewer, we have two ideas. If humor leaves the Finnish viewer, it might do so earlier (around lines 73 to 80) when Safer says "Finns glory in their isolation"[1] but we think it mostly departs later (by line 331) when Safer laughs, according to many Finns, inappropriately and too much. From a Finnish view, these scenes with others build to a cumulative point an uninformed, exaggerated, and negative interpretation of Finnishness.

Many initial formulations included reference to this sequence of emotions and were quite brief and to the point. A 23-year-old female said: "First it made me laugh but when I think that this is the image the others are given of Finland, it makes me sort of angry." Or from another Finnish viewer, "First it was funny, but eventually it started to be annoying." Or again, in an understated way, "It made me laugh at first, but then it made me a little bit irritated."

This Finnish discourse expresses both humor and anger, often—but not always—played together ambivalently. In any event, Finnish views of the video and the discourse about it render it verbally as both funny and aggravating. How can that be?

A FINNISH FORM OF COMMUNICATION: IRONY, SATIRE, AND SELF-DEPRECATING JOKES

Unlike the US discourse, which presumes, for the most part, that *60 Minutes* shows factual news, the Finnish discourse included a prominent feature that framed the episode, or parts of the episode, as a joke. A Finnish viewer put it this way:

> I could see in my mind's eye how the persons that were interviewed chuckled inside: Let's give this foreign reporter wilder stories than he ever dreamed of.

This is a very telling formulation for it presumes a way of seeing and hearing Finnish speakers as chuckling inside. Perhaps this is not evident on the surface to outsiders, but it is understood this way immediately by some Finns. This cultural knowledge provides a way of framing the episode—and sequential structures within it—with at least some of its contents and performances becoming a joke. In fact, Finns portray some of it as "wild stories," exaggerated reports for humorous effect, with the butt of the joke being Finns themselves.[2] There is concern, however, that all of this escapes the notice of the correspondent, Safer, the journalist Schultz, and all those millions of American viewers. We Finns are laughing, but are they taking this seriously!?

The complexity of features in Finnish satire and jokes plays on these primary dimensions of the serious and the playful, as well as the dimension of insider and outsider knowledge. Sometimes the Finnish discourse referred simply and directly to a particularly humorous part. For example, a 24-year-old female found Knutas to be very funny (on lines 322–329):

> The interviewed man [Knutas] was very funny actually (e.g., I love you is only said when your spouse is just about to die).

Knutas' humor is deemed particularly funny in Finland by Finnish standards, and sometimes more easily so by men than women. Others commented generally about the clip as a whole being a funny treatment of Finnish culture. A 25-year-old female said:

> I liked the clip as it was and I have myself sarcastically thought of Finland as the "suffering culture"—tuskakulttuuri—where your value is measured by how much you have suffered.

When "Tango Finlandia" was mentioned to a middle-aged Finnish woman, however, she reluctantly acknowledged having seen it and hearing about it repeatedly. She did not smile when she called the program "an example of Finnish dark humor."

A familiar genre is activated in this discourse, one in which humor is a central—if not always appreciated—theme. Sometimes viewers wondered why this was being produced by Finnish speakers for foreigners, for it can play on the suffering or darker side of Finnish life.

Finnish Self-deprecating Humor (Irony and Sarcasm)

There is a special genre of humor active here and there in the video, at least according to some Finnish commentators. Because Finns do care so deeply about what foreigners think of them, there is concern about others' negative evaluations of Finns. This has even become a familiar part of a Finnish cultural conversation (e.g., Sallinen-Kuparinen, 1986). For example, the US discourse earlier portrays Finns as inexpressive, sad, and shy. This stereotypical impression of Finns by Americans is something fairly commonly known in Finland. Further, this rather negative evaluation of Finns by others is used by some Finns as a criticism of Finnishness and by others as a playful statement about who Finns are. This creates a kind of self-deprecating humor, even if the materials played with, and the standard of judgment applied to them, is being imported from elsewhere. When this judgment starts forming bases of belief by Finns as a part of their Finnishness, the statements can create a kind of dark side of Finnishness, where others' views of Finns cast a dark shadow over Finnish views of themselves. For these and other cultural reasons, this complex genre of humor can be not only complicated, but irritating. As one Finnish viewer said:

> I don't know why Finnish people try to destroy their image so desperately.

Note that the concern expressed most prominently in the Finnish discourse is a concern with Finnish identity and how it is being formulated by others AND by Finns. Because of the complexity of issues involved, this play between humorous and serious matters, insider and outsider images, sometimes is difficult to sort through, especially for Finnish viewers. As a result, and at times, Finnish viewers themselves may not be sure if this televised episode can be (or should be considered) a joke. A 36-year-old Finnish female wondered whether or not this episode was serious or playful. Her formulation even invokes the very self-deprecating image it questions and wonders whether it is funny or not:

> Was this a serious attempt to describe Finns? As geriatric tango shufflers with paralyzed faces?

And if this was funny or was supposed to be funny, it probably was so in one way to Finns and in quite another to Americans:

> If this was a joke, I would just laugh with the Americans. Maybe in different parts but laugh.

A 45-year-old woman expressed concern that the special Finnish nature of the humor would not be understood in the United States, and therefore would be considered much more seriously than it should be:

> This is a special kind of irony of Finns geared to themselves. To us it is very funny, but if you think somebody would take it seriously . . . that's terrible.

Again, if this was a joke, there is concern about who gets it and an acknowledgment that, as one 24-year-old Finnish female put it, "Maybe only Finns understand the jokes."

The Jokes as True and False

A pronounced theme throughout the Finnish discourse draws attention to this "Tango Finlandia" episode as being both true and false. Some commentators pointed to the parts of the video that were factual, as when a 25-year-old male said, "The 'don't notice me, please' part was as accurate as it gets" (in lines 56–62). Others worried that the Americans would take the whole thing seriously. "Americans tend to take things like this as the truth, but this clip should be taken with humor." The point here is that the clip includes some truth, yet it is not just true and serious, but also playful and exaggerated. This point was made in the Finnish discourse about the televised text:

> The film was a funny mixture of fact and fiction or exaggeration and reality. It was full of very common stereotypes, but in such an exaggerated way that it made us seem ridiculous and pathetic. So, the same thing that made it accurate made it seem to be a clip of comedy.

A 30-year-old male put it this way:

> This clip is a caricature of Finland. Actually, the interpretation given, and the image given are caricatural, even if much of the "raw material" is very accurate.

This Finnish discourse provides us with a complicated reading of the televisual text. How can it be that it is both serious and playful, is understood one way by insiders and most likely another way by those on the outside, and how can this episode be both true and not true? These are puzzling questions and complicated dynamics.

Boundaries of Finnish Jokes

Our effort to understand this complex discourse is aided here by Keith Basso's (1979) theory of imitative jokes. Based upon careful ethnographic analyses of Western Apaches' imitative jokes about "the whiteman," Basso explicates a structural form for understanding imitative jokes.

Imitative jokes, he claims, are built when a primary, serious text of everyday life is made into a secondary, exaggerated, and playful text. Primary texts are "strips of 'serious' behavior," as Basso puts it, which "furnish the raw materials from which joking performances are fashioned" (1979, p. 41). To know a primary text, one must be immersed in the routine way of life that makes it relevant. For the Western Apache, this meant knowing about specific interactions with "the whiteman," such as Apache children dealing with "white" teachers in schools, or with "whiteman" doctors in health clinics, and the like in other social occasions. Secondary texts created as primary texts like these are subjected to a playfully exaggerated performance. This, according to Basso, follows two principles. One is a principle of contrast: select points of contrast between your way and others' ways. Then, implement the distortion principle: create an exaggerated image and embellish it for humorous effect. The key is to get others to pretend during the joking performance "that the secondary text is a primary one, and that the whole affair is not a mock-up of some precedent reality, but the reality itself" (Basso, 1979, p. 41). As Apache jokers exaggerate a "whiteman's" greeting, participants can smile and laugh, throwing into relief this familiar way of acting. The key to interpreting the joke is knowing both what the serious strips of behavior indeed are and knowing how they are being creatively exaggerated for humorous effect.

For Finnish participants, the form is not imitating another, but one's own, cultural ways. The playful performance builds upon strips of everyday life like walking public streets, sitting on a bus, dancing the tango, when to say "I love you," and the like. Then, an exaggerated performance of this cultural reality is performed for humorous effect. Finnish viewers, of course, are knowledgeable about these Finnish ways, and are thus in a position to know both the everyday basis of a primary text and to recognize a playful performance or exaggeration of it. In other words, Finnish viewers understand the relations between the primary and secondary texts in their self-deprecating jokes and just how this is being performed by the Finns in the video.

American viewers, generally, do not. The jokes simply cannot work for them if they do not have access, in Basso's terms, to the primary texts, the everyday life of Finns.

If we use these ideas to reflect upon the televised episode and the Finnish discourse about it, we are invited to examine primary strips of everyday Finnish life that are presumably serious. Such things include, in addition to what was noted earlier, social relations with, evaluations by, and differences from foreigners. On the bases of some of these relations, Finnish people know that they are often portrayed in English, especially by Americans, as shy and perhaps silent or inexpressive people. Consider that the ways others see Finns provide some of the primary "raw materials" for the Finnish joking performance. This is done especially by Knutas on lines 40–47 and 55–71, which presumes a knowing contrast between a popular US American extroversion and talkativeness and a Finnish introversion and respectful silence. Further, it presumes that what Knutas is doing is performing an exaggerated version of these Finnish qualities. He builds his playfulness, then, through this contrast of American and Finnish ways and through this distortion of Finnish ways, thus exaggerating the shy, silent, and inexpressive qualities presumed by American viewers to be Finnish.

A difficulty with this joking performance, of course, is mentioned in the Finnish discourse about the televised episode. As a joke, it includes, in Finnish terms, both "fact and fiction," "exaggeration and reality," "a caricature" and an "accurate" picture. In the words of our model, it includes both a secondary text of distortions and exaggerations of Finnish reality, as well as primary texts of serious behavior. One telling example is the Finnish male who approvingly noted the accuracy and perhaps the seriousness of the "don't notice me, please" feature. This was perhaps evident in a secondary text as when Knutas provided an embellished version of the "horrifying thought" of someone wanting to talk with him (on lines 55–71).[3] Yet what may have been, and probably was, missed by many US Americans was that this was, to a significant degree, a self-caricature, a distorted version of Finnishness for humorous purposes. Knutas' comments about having "to engage in a conversation" (lines 59–60) and the experienced "horror" of this cue are playful exaggerations to Finnish viewers. Note, however, from a Finnish view that it is not really "inexpressiveness" that is at stake here, for that is a bit of a US American way of exaggerating. What is at stake is the seriousness in being respectfully silent (hiljaisuus) or alone in your thoughts (omissa oloissaan), and similarly it is not really horrifying to talk with strangers, just not preferable that one produce "unnecessary talk" (a Finnish phrase) with someone on a bus. As a result, the joke becomes funny as a self-deprecating caricature, with this being based upon a more serious side of Finnishness and social conduct.

The concerns expressed by Finnish viewers about this episode derive also partly from the social context of the mediated event. In the episode itself, Knutas is sitting on a public park bench talking with a foreigner, Morley Safer. Both are part of a televised text in which Finland is being presented to US Americans. The concern is that Finnish viewers know how to interpret this whole thing as a playful joke, for it plays with serious things that are both true and false, but US Americans will not get this. The Finnish discourse thus expressed worry or concern that the US Americans, apparently like Safer, will take the exaggerated image as the truth. A 30-year-old Finnish man put it this way:

> [This is] very accurate from the point of view of [the] Finnish sense of self-irony. Very inaccurate if you want to "teach" something about Finland to representatives of other cultures.

A 26-year-old Finnish female commented:

> This must be some kind of a joke—big time—with a bad taste.

A 45-year-old Finnish female said:

> This is a special kind of irony of Finns geared to themselves. To us it is very funny, but if you think somebody would take it seriously, that's terrible.

Again, this is apparently just what some saw Safer doing: taking the humorous parts as serious facts and laughing when he should be pondering the seriousness of it all. While many commented that Safer was indeed likeable, and they even enjoyed his "chatty manner of interviewing," there was a difficulty expressed with some of his reactions. A 34-year-old female put it this way:

Safer's hilarious laughing was such a contradiction with the theme he presented. He did not realize the tragedy and seriousness of this Finnish feature. He did not find any positive things in it.

We are certain she is referring in part to Safer's laughter at line 330, which is prompted by Knutas' comment that you could say "I love you" "once in a lifetime," perhaps when your "spouse is on her deathbed" (lines 323–327). Safer has somehow, from this Finnish view, stepped out of bounds. We hear deep meaning in the woman's Finnish discourse here. With it, we think it is not just that Safer laughs too much, which perhaps from a Finnish view he does, but that he does not see the seriousness, "the tragedy and seriousness," that is the Finnish basis for the laughter. Here, at this point in the video clip, Finns can be prompted to say and feel with Knutas that "it's not funny." In Finnish, at this point, one would likely say, "Se ei ole naurun asia" (It is not a laughing matter). There is a complicated cultural reality at the base of this reaction. Safer, and perhaps American viewers, have missed or have no access to the primary Finnish texts that make it so.

One feature of this Finnish reality is keyed to the immediate social relation between Knutas and Safer and the gradual realization (building from at least line 318) that Safer does not understand what is at stake in Knutas' Finnish, joking performance. By laughing "hilariously" or too much, perhaps even out of control by Finnish standards, he has sent the message that he doesn't really understand. This is a problem. A second feature derives from the first. Because Safer is eventually seen as not fully understanding, he cannot be seen as a full party to the joke, and as a result, he is seen to be no longer laughing WITH Finns, as Finns understand the joke, but AT them. This is unacceptable. As one Finnish commentator said, "One thing is never allowed: That a stranger makes fun of your culture" (cf. Philipsen, 2000).

A third feature of Finnish reality is at stake in the joke. It also relates to the primary text brought to the fore by Knutas' comments here. Knutas says one may say "minä rakastan sinua" (translated into English as "I love you" but not its equivalent) only "once in a lifetime" (line 323). This claim is heard by many Finns as playful and not literal and brings to the discussion the Finnish concern that we Finns, especially Finnish men, do not express emotions enough. One often hears that Finnish men "rarely talk or kiss." This is sometimes mentioned as a reason for difficulties in interpersonal relationships and for a rather high rate of divorce, currently at about 50 percent. For Finns, these parts of reality, of course, are not something to be laughed at. A fourth feature of serious reality at stake in this joke is the Finnish belief about a Finnish style of communicating: we do express our emotions in a Finnish way quite well, thank you, and we do so often nonverbally. We don't say what we feel as much as we show it. In fact, speaking feelings verbally can be redundant and may even call them into doubt! Why say "I love you" to one who already knows it?

Clearly, there is an interpretive depth and seriousness at play in the joke, and in the episode generally, with a deep serious berg beneath the playful ice of Knutas' joke. At the heart of it is a deep sense of Finnishness, a Finnish view that Americans likely missed.

FINNISHNESS AS FEATURED IN THIS MEDIATED WORLD: THE POSITIVE IN IT

As imitative jokes and playful texts play on contrasts between worlds, they may be heard to implicate deeper cultural meanings, beliefs, and values; about what a person is (and should be); how one can (and should) act; and how one can (and should) feel. In the Finnish discourse here under study, both in and about the video text, we hear several implicit premises that we will now make explicit. Our claim is that these premises, akin to the ones grounding Knutas' joke, form a key part of the Finnish cultural bedrock in the discourse presented earlier.

A Finnish model of personhood is active in this discourse, and in fact was praised in the discourse some Finnish viewers produced about the clip. Consider the following instances staking a claim comparatively to a distinctly Finnish identity. All acknowledge again that the way you (foreigners generally) see us is not the way we see ourselves, and we are, by our own standards, good and righteous people.

> From a 23-year-old female: I have to admit that we Finns are like that, if you want to see us like that, but we don't think ourselves to be "bad."

The Finnish concept of politeness and friendliness is somewhat different from the American—or at least it manifests itself in another way.

> From a 26-year-old female from Jyväskylä: The Finns are a bit more quiet and introverted, but the context and standards and expectations in the clip were too American.

> From another 26-year-old female from Jyväskylä: There is nothing wrong with being a private person, even if Americans aren't!

In these verbal comments we now hear a set of Finnish cultural propositions and premises. We can formulate some of them as follows:

1) We Finns are at heart realistic. We know who we are, no more and no less. We don't try to be something we are not.
2) We are very aware that we are different from others. You call us inexpressive, shy, and the like. I guess you can do that, if you like, for you know English better than we, but we don't necessarily see ourselves that way, especially not in Finnish.

3) We know that others misinterpret us, usually in negative terms, like Finns are not talkative or are not extroverted. In fact, we often say about ourselves what we are *not* in the negative form, saying things like we are not Swedes, not Russians, or not talkative.
4) Conversely, we do not speak about what is obvious; thus we do not say what we are, which we all already know. As a result, when we speak, we speak in the negative about what we are not, saying nothing about what we know ourselves to be. Thus, we know the negative statements of others about us are not entirely true as what we think ourselves to be.
5) We can, and perhaps at times should, be different from what we think we are, both among ourselves and when interacting with foreigners.
6) We know some others' ways of doing things are more talkative, and this at times seems to us to be superficial. We know we are deeper and can communicate better in our own ways, if not in their ways, which for the most part we don't want. So, as a 23-year-old female said: "Despite all, I'm very happy to be a Finn."

In summary, the Finnish discourse in and about the televised episode explored here is deeply aggravated, and at times formulated, around a deep emotional ambivalence, both laughing and getting irritated or angry. The laughter is framed by reference to a distinct Finnish everyday genre of self-deprecating humor, irony, and satire. For this form of humor to work, serious aspects of everyday Finnish life must be presumed and commonly known, including this form of humor itself and how it playfully distorts serious realities. Anger is discussed when the play (the secondary exaggerated text) is misunderstood as serious (the serious primary text) or when distorted and caricatured Finnish conduct is mistaken as actual truths about Finns. The Finnish discourse thus straddles its cultural borders; it plays at the boundaries of humor, for the model of identity at play is both serious and playful, factual and fictional, yet known properly only by insiders not outsiders. As such, the discourse crafts and affirms unique premises about Finnish personhood, actions, relations, and feelings, in contrast to unknowing others.[4]

NOTES

1 The visual images shown here carry powerful messages that, according to Finnish viewers' reports, absurdly and erroneously link reindeer rides in Lapland, arctic features of Finnish composer Jean Sibelius, and the sauna as something painful (!) to a national Finnish character.
2 For example, around lines 41, 61, 69, and 327.
3 The "don't notice me, please" theme also can be seen in primary texts, as when Finnish people's proper "street or bus faces" were being shown.
4 For a detailed look at Finnish claims of "American superficiality" see Carbaugh, 2005.

Chapter 6
Enlarging the Cultural Discourse
Coding Finnish "Quietude" in Everyday Contexts

> Being alone does not mean loneliness but a withdrawal into one's chosen peace.
>
> To the Finn quietness and the hospitality which takes others into consideration are not mutually exclusive. Finnish literature's most beautiful portrayals of friendship and love present the silence of being together. A firm relationship with another is not brought about by exchanged words but by way of shared unspoken gestures.
>
> (Markku Koivusalo, 1999, pp. 51, 50)

A Finnish exchange student, Tiina, was attending high school in Iowa in America's heartland. She was living with a friendly host family who wanted to show her all they could of their home town and its surrounding environs. As Tiina recounted her time in America, she mentioned her dear friends and exciting events she had seen, including college basketball games. However, she also puzzled over many features of American culture, including its eating habits, relations between boys and girls, the curriculum of the high school, television programs, and fan behavior at sporting events. Yet none of these recollections animated—nor agitated—her nearly as much as a particular dynamic that occurred when she was with her host family.

Tiina described the dynamic like this: As a part of the family's weekly routine, typically on a Sunday, members would go for a ride in their car across the Iowan countryside. As was part of this custom, the family would engage in social conversation while traveling together. The Finnish student enjoyed the ride, was quite comfortable listening to the conversation and watching the towns and fields pass by. Yet, after a while in the car together, after traveling through several cornfields and conversations, the father would turn to Tiina and ask, "Is everything OK?" The first time she was asked, the question startled Tiina. Caught off guard she replied simply, "Yes." The car continued rolling along, the conversation would pick up again and turn to other matters, with her attentive to it but feeling no need to be verbally engaged in it. Eventually, the father would ask again, with some concern, "Are you sure you are alright?" Growing a bit more uncomfortable, Tiina replied, again, "Yes." During some of the drives, the father would, according to Tiina, become angry and demand to know why she was being so quiet and not saying anything! Tiina reported that these events were difficult for her, made her very uncomfortable, and were nearly impossible for her to understand. She was deeply perplexed.

As the young woman recalled this dynamic, she expressed bewilderment about it. She reported how time after time, and over time, the matter escalated, culminating too often, and uncomfortably, in the father's exasperated question, through a raised voice, "Are you sure everything is OK?" with her replying in an equal amount of dismay, "Yes"; or his asking, "Why aren't you saying anything?" and her replying "I don't have anything to say." Tiina was left thinking, "Why wouldn't everything be OK? Why am I being pressured to talk all the time?"

This customary event of this family, like the events in the "Tango Finlandia" document, brings to light a particular kind of question: What activity is presumably at play when people gather socially and at times speak together? What preferences or obligations does it bring to a social scene? And, in turn, and similarly, what activity is presumably getting done when people are together in silence? What preferences are woven into such scenes? This chapter builds on the cultural discourses people used in the previous chapters by responding to those questions. The special focus here is cultural conceptions of speaking and silence. We shall see that people, like Tiina and her host family, not only use language in cultural ways, but are silent in cultural ways as well. We will gain access to these expressive ways through cultural terms that give these events, of speaking and silence, their particular shapes and meanings. We will see further how each helps shape the other, both between and within special communication codes.

COMMUNICATION CODES THROUGH CULTURAL TERMS

Every communication system includes terms, symbols, and gestures that are used to comment upon that system. These have been variously understood as a meta-discourse (Craig, 1999a, 1999b; Taylor, 1986), as a meta-language (Lucy, 1992), as language action verbs or meta-pragmatic terms (Verschueren, 1985), and as key terms (Wierzbicka, 1997, 2003). One subset of these meta-communicative phenomena can be understood as cultural terms for communicative action—that is, as terms and phrases that are used prominently and routinely by people to characterize communication practices that are significant and important to them. For example, Mary Garrett (1993) has analyzed a complex form of talk in ancient China that is identified in its English translation as "pure talk." Leslie Baxter (1993) has identified two principal, yet differently valued, media for communication in an academic institution, which are discussed as "talking things through" and "putting it in writing." Similarly, Brad Hall and Matsumi Noguchi (1995) identified "kenson" as a Japanese term that identifies for its users practical forms of common sense. Most recently, Tamar Katriel (2004) has insightfully explored "soul talk, talking straight, and talk radio" as three communication forms that have given shape and meaning to twentieth-century Israeli society.[1] In each of these studies, the author explored indigenous practices of communication by identifying cultural terms for them; observed routine enactments of the practices so identified; and investigated the various meanings, premises, and rules for these events.[2]

Like these previous studies, the analyses in this chapter are focused on parts of cultural discourse that focuses on communication itself (Carbaugh, 1989, 2005; Carbaugh, Gibson, and Milburn, 1997). Earlier studies have identified such terms and practices as central features in cultural discourses about speaking and personhood (Carbaugh, 1988, pp. 121–184; Wilkins, 2005, 2009), with Philipsen (1992, pp. 123–141; 1997, pp. 142–146) emphasizing the importance of these phenomena in the formulation of speech codes and Philipsen, Coutu, and Covarrubias (2005) discussing their potential value in formulations of culturally discursive dynamics. The analytic objective is to hear first culturally distinctive communication practices, and then within them, deep cultural meanings about communication itself, the nature of persons, social relationships, emotions, and dwelling in nature.[3]

The goals of the chapter are to describe and interpret the social life of communication broadly through the cultural frames of those who live it, while developing a general theoretical approach for such ethnographic and comparative inquiry. In earlier studies, authors have found by focusing on a symbolic cluster of terms, as those we analyzed earlier in Chapters 3 and 4, an analyst helps bring into view a range of communication practices, including the actions those practices are used to do. The main cluster of terms and practices of concern to us here is avowedly a right, proper, and natural way to be, an ideology of interpersonal life identified by Tiina and used by speakers of Finnish.

A "NATURAL WAY TO BE" ("LUONTEVA TAPA OLLA"): EXPRESSING FINNISHNESS

There is a special kind of social practice identified variously in Finnish as "luonteva tapa olla" or "että on luontevaa"; the phrases are translated here as "a natural, normal way to be" or "being natural with ease." The phrase was used by Jan Knutas (on line 121, 121a), the Finnish media personality, as he was talking to Morley Safer. The phrase is an effort by Knutas to characterize something about Finnish comportment to Safer.

116) <u>SAFER</u>: it strikes me uh traveling around this country that (.)
    a) O*len matkustellut täällä*

117) people are **terribly** shy (.)
118)   particularly **the men**
   a)   *ja etenkin miehet vaikuttavat ujoilta.*
119) KNUTAS: ((Voiceover))
120) among ourselves
121)   we think that is the natural way to be.
   a)   *Ajattelemme, että on luontevaa*
122)   not to sort of (.)stick out
   a)   *olla erottumatta joukosta.*
123) It's easy to see that from coming from another country *hh
   a)   *Muualta tulevat*
124)   you think of it as shyness
   a)   *pitävät sitä ujoutena*
125)   and it probably is **yes**
   a)   *Sitä se varmaankin on*

In these lines, Knutas is saying something about Finnishness, with this being related to what was mentioned by Safer on lines 116–118 and earlier. The verbal line drawn here, like in hundreds of Finnish to English translations before it, links a Finnish "natural way to be" to "shyness" (in American English). Eventually, Knutas, as other Finnish speakers before him, rather begrudgingly relents to this linkage on lines 124 and 125. But notice his hedged phrasing on those lines as "you think of it" that way (line 124), and "it probably is" (line 125), suggesting the English term "shyness" may not quite capture the Finnish meaning of things (as in its root Finnish word, "ujo," on line 124a). The quick stamping of the English word "shyness" onto what Knutas describes as "natural" obscures other Finnish meanings at play here. In other words, Knutas, rather than echoing Safer's earlier words and meanings (from the stance of a US discourse), is alternately echoing Finnish primary texts, practices, and meanings (from the stance of a Finnish discourse). Again, within a Finnish discourse, Knutas is not simply echoing the American comment, but is more deeply echoing a parallel Finnish voice. Hearing, at this point, not just a US American voice, but now a parallel voice, we can further develop the "dual echoing structure" active in this and other places in the document. Recall in Chapters 3 and 4, we emphasized the first echo with an American accent; in Chapter 5 and here we emphasize the second echo, the Finnish accent. It is those latter, "natural" Finnish sounds, and the related practices they invoke, we now seek to understand.[4] Our focus is on the Finnish practices and premises identified by Finns as "luonteva tapa olla" and to render them as Finnish does, as something more than or other than "shyness" in English.

This "natural" ("luonteva, luonnollinen") way of being is presumed for the conduct of some Finnish primary social texts and is linked through uses of Finnish investigated later with a range of related terms, including prominently "olla omissa oloissaan" (being undisturbed in one's thoughts) and "mietiskellä" (being contemplative and thoughtful). There are other terms associated with these which will be considered later, but these three phrases identify the main symbolic territory of interpersonal life of concern in this chapter, mainly because these are the Finnish terms used by Finnish speakers in our corpus to identify this feature of Finnishness, that is, "a natural way to be." (The terms are used on lines 25a, 42a, 43a, and 121a, for example.)[5] And, of course, these are not the only features of Finnishness any more than "straight talk" is of the Israeli Sabra (Katriel, 2004), "kenson" is in Japan (Hall and Noguchi, 1995), or "sharing feelings" is to Americans (Carbaugh, 1989). Yet like "straight talk," "kenson," and "sharing feelings," a "natural way of being" is active on some cultural occasions, in this case for some Finns, and by focusing on this and the features of the cultural scene it makes relevant, we can understand some of its shapes and meanings. And so we are asking: What is this "natural way of being" that Knutas identifies? What Finnish discourse is being so identified and practiced with these phrases through these practices?

"OLLA OMISSA OLOISSAAN" (A VALUE IN BEING UNDISTURBED IN ONE'S THOUGHTS)

A Finnish man, Heikki, was describing a typical social routine in his life: riding the train from his home town to a city where he was attending courses at the university. Speaking in English, but using some Finnish terms, he described his time on the train to his interlocutor, Michael:

Heikki: I have moments where I actually decide at home that I am going to mietiskellä [be thoughtful] or olla omissa +oloissani [remain undisturbed] and really don't feel like talking with anybody. And then that's what I do.
Michael: But now, when you feel that way, do you ever have to say it, to get the message across [to others, that you want to "olla omissa oloissasi"]?
Heikki: No. No.
Michael: Everybody knows what you mean?
Heikki: Definitely. The message is quite clear. If I just don't say it, and I just don't talk, it is totally normal. Nobody will come and question me.

In this exchange, Heikki is describing a kind of action, in Finnish terms, as "mietiskellä" and as "olla omissa oloissaan." He suggests these are actions he plans to do while on the train. He can do this very action when he doesn't "really feel like talking with anybody." Further, Heikki makes clear that these actions are part of a taken-for-granted cultural scene, an unspoken script for nonverbal action, or a code that is presumably active among people while on the train. After all, according to him, "the message is quite clear." When doing this in this way and in similar scenes (like on the bus), these actions are presumably quite natural, even, as Heikki puts it, "totally normal." In other words, following Heikki's comments here as he crafts this Finnish scene, he wants us to understand that people can be quiet, and that this is natural. When there is no speaking, "everybody knows" something important is going on. What is going on in Heikki's view is prevalent, valued, and can be described not as "just sitting" but through the Finnish terms "olla omissa oloissaan" and "mietiskellä."

When speaking to users of English, especially users of American English, Heikki and others emphasize that these actions are important to one's well-being and are natural ways people engage in their everyday worlds routinely. Note that these terms, therefore, identify and declare productive cultural activities. When alone or together in these ways, something positively natural and good is happening. This is an important point. Why? Some observers from elsewhere, where talk is deemed central to most cultural activity, have concluded about this and similar Finnish scenes that "nothing is happening" because "no one is saying anything." Note the negatives, "nothing" and "no one" at work in this identification. This kind of interpretation is, of course, different from the one Heikki supplies. To him, and the "everybody" he invokes, there is valued, efficacious social action here; rather than "nothing," there is indeed something important going on. We shall see eventually how silence and quietude can set the stage for important Finnish scenes of social life, where talk is unnecessary, even intrusive.[6]

What is Heikki saying, then, when he claims that performing these actions themselves makes "the message ... quite clear"? What taken-for-granted version of cultural life is being expressed? One way of responding to these questions is to remind ourselves that the Finish cultural scene here is being erected on the cultural premise that there is a natural desire to be quiet and contemplative, to be undisturbed in one's own thoughts.

The phrase "olla omissa oloissaan," is a key cultural term in expressing this Finnish feature. As used by Heikki and others, it identifies and gives shape to a distinctly, albeit natural, form of Finnish action. Some of the significance of this term and action was described in detail by Marja, a middle-aged Finnish woman:

> Omissa oloissaan is a perfectly legitimate, positive state of being, to be actually undisturbed. It's just a natural need for being alone, undisturbed in your own thoughts, and sort of in your own territory undisturbed. We respect that. People want to be omissa oloissaan so that means that we respect that, because we know that everybody wants to be that way, at least once in a while.

During a conversation with Mika, he also emphasized the need and desire for such activity. He described making plans with his friend for an upcoming holiday:

> I will spend a week in the summer cottage in order to be "omissa oloissaan" [to spend time by myself]. Those present will include me, and perhaps my friend. The goal is to let other people know you want to be alone without anybody disturbing you. This is a very commonly used word. It describes a state of mind, when you want to calm down, get away from the hectic life and be alone with your thoughts.

As Tiina, Heikki, Marja, and Mika discuss their social life, they create a special place for activities they describe as "olla omissa oloissaan." We can interpret some of the meanings of this term and some of the features in this Finnish action as follows: in interpersonal life, there are moments of quietude; these are natural or normal; at times, we strongly desire and want these moments; in them, we are undisturbed, calm, in our own thoughts; we take for granted that these moments are natural and desirable.

In social scenes, one can be identified as "in one's thoughts" and thus should be "undisturbed." But this action is not just attached to an individual. Socially engaged quietude can lend an integral defining form to larger social occasions. When people are together on a bus or train with family or friends, it can set the stage for a full cultural event. Marja put it this way: "You can be alone in your thoughts, in your own mental space, but you can also be together with others. Sometimes we are in a room together with family or friends and we can do this together." When my wife and I (DC) have visited with our Finnish friends, we have found our delightful and engaging discussions interspersed occasionally with these moments of quietude. Over the years—and this took some considerable time for us to appreciate, coming, as we did, from a "talking culture"—we have come to enjoy these moments immensely, alone in our thoughts for a while, able to be calm and quiet with others, together, for several minutes on end.

Scenes such as these bring with them local meanings and morals about politeness, thoughtfulness, and privacy that are to be respected. Marja put it this way:

> [W]e like our territory undisturbed . . . When you are keeping your distance from others then you are not intruding [on] somebody else's privacy, but you are not allowing anybody to intrude [on] your privacy either. It's like having these big bubbles that nobody is intruding. Keep the distance.

This matter can be expressed as one of respect. As Mervi put it:

> "I associate privacy with respecting other people. We appreciate when people are not talking but listening. We Finns do not think it is impolite to be just quiet in a group. I see privacy as a positive and associate privacy with space which people need for living. We might even enjoy being alone and that is why we

do not want to interrupt others by talking all the time. Privacy is being alone in a good way.

Perhaps this is what the tango singer, Arja Koriseva, alluded to as recognizing a respectful "wall" of privacy among people, affirming it, and not just presuming a verbal link is preferable to it (line 104).

"Being alone in a good way" is a social achievement and a matter of social tact, as one exercises a proper propensity for silence or, from another angle, a proper verbal reserve. In doing so, one honors one's own and others' privacy. In the process, meaningful Finnish action is linked to a proper care of self and others, thereby protecting all social actors from unwanted intrusions. As a middle-aged Finnish woman, Pirjo, put it:

> We want to protect ourselves from the unknown but we also want to protect the other person from the unknown. We want to respect the other person's privacy and in a way make sure that she or he really wants to talk. In Finland, it's OK not to talk all the time and in my opinion most of the Finns don't feel awkward when nobody talks. We don't feel that we have to talk just for talking (in order to avoid silence) and we can feel comfortable when nobody is talking. We are comfortable with quietness.

One can be alone in various ways, physically and mentally.

> If you are "omissa oloissasi" you are quite often alone, but it doesn't need to be that way. "Olla yksin" (to be by oneself) is this, but something else. It can be you are physically alone but not mentally alone, as when the telephone is ringing. It can also mean that you are mentally alone but not physically alone, as when one has marital problems and is "yksin" [alone], mentally alone, in a marriage. Here, it means that there is no comrade-ship, you are emotionally alone, as one can be alone in the middle of a busy street. Or in a noisy household, for instance, if there is a black sheep who's alone.

Being alone, then, can carry various meanings of physical, mental, and socioemotional aloneness. In the extreme, these can create a form of isolation, especially in the frame of social punishment, as a "black sheep" or being in the "dog house" illustrates. Being alone, then, in a good way is to draw attention to the positive, undisturbed form of physical, mental, and social aloneness. This provides for the personal and social good.

This cultural form of social life is essential for one's sense of well-being and also for one's proper development. A Finnish mother described coming home from a hard day at work:

> If one has done something that has been strenuous, then of course one would like to have a moment of that, and usually people respect it. Even children are

taught to respect it when parents come home from work. I don't know if all parents do it, but then children let them breathe for awhile before attacking them.

Marja lamented how people today and children in particular can become overloaded with a fast-paced routine and calendar:

> Children nowadays are taken from one thing to the next and then they are rarely allowed to be omissa oloissaan, which means that they would just sit down and figure things out alone and by themselves, then they don't have to have everything preprogrammed for them. This time alone is a source of creativity for them, because then children will start figuring things out about themselves. It's also like meditation, some of it is meditation. That way, you get refined in peace of mind and balance and sort things out. Just resting. This can provide one moment of concentration, one moment of focusing your mental energy, sort of inwards. This is a moment of rest and reflection . . . We can call this lots of things, but we often do not verbalize it. When there is a need, you just do it. And if we see somebody, we see the need and then we respect it. It's one of those body-language things.

On the basis of these comments and practices, we can understand several additional Finnish premises for "being alone in a good way." This is indeed a cultural form of practice, giving shape to many possible social scenes involving public, educational, familial, and friendship interactions; these scenes allow a proper privacy for participants, giving relationships a social distance where it is due; the form serves a protective function, giving a social territory for each which is to be honored socially or not to be intruded upon; the distance and protection provided by the form are necessary for one's well-being (as an adult) and one's development (as a child). Consequently, this form and these premises give shape to actions in a polite, natural, Finnish way, and are, therefore, to be respected.

Of course, any practice can occur in an excessive way, and this is also the case for "being alone in a good way." One Finnish friend reminded us of this:

> If someone wants to be constantly "omissa oloissaan," one would get worried, although nowadays it is so rare to spend time alone, as the culture dictates the pace of social tempo. It is accepted for an employee or a mother to sometimes be "omissa oloissaan" and in these cases this activity has a very positive meaning. If an unsocial person constantly wants to be "omissa oloissaan," it has a negative meaning.

The idea that one should honor moments of quietude, both alone and with others, does not imply that one is or should be pathologically quiet (or as Safer would have it, to be "clinically shy" or "terminally melancholy"). Sometimes such a person was referred to as a "hermit" or one who spends too much time alone. Too much of a good thing can be detrimental.

There is also apparently a slight variation in the ways this practice plays into different social scenes and institutions. For example, it may be the case that this form of quietude, when active and recounted, casts matters as ones of privacy in public scenes, for example, with neighbors and colleagues; while the same practice of quietude may cast matters less as private and more as a necessary protection of personal space in more intimate spheres, that is, with family or friends. In other words, this form of quietude is linked directly to privacy and protection across social scenes (as Koriseva explains, we have "like a wall" of protection here), yet concerns of privacy may assume greater importance in public scenes than in more intimate settings.

These practices and commentary have cast the kinds of activities involved when "being alone in a good way." Some of these include related cultural acts, such as "figuring things out by yourself," "a form of meditation," "one moment of concentration," "resting," "peace of mind and balance," "focusing your mental energy," and "reflection." In Finnish, there is a term that identifies these various related actions: "mietiskellä." These related practices can occur when one is "undisturbed, alone in one's thoughts." In fact, being alone in one's thoughts, quiet and silent ("hiljaisuus"), is necessary for "mietiskellä" (contemplation, meditation, reflection). From the Finnish view, then, what is this related practice? What makes it important?

MIETISKELLÄ, MIETISKELEVÄISYYS (THOUGHTFULNESS): CONTEMPLATION, MEDITATION, REFLECTION

As many others, Marja's eyes danced as she obviously delighted in describing this form of Finnish activity:

> Mietiskellä is almost like . . . meditation. It is deep. Usually when you meditate, there is some sort of a physical condition about your environment. Of course some people can do it in the middle of a horrendous situation with lots of noise, but most people can't. But definitely, when you are doing mietiskellä, when you are doing that, there is some kind of peace and quiet, be it in your head or also in your head and the environment. I think for most people it requires this "omissa oloissaan" definitely.

The activity brings together two important features in the expression of Finnishness: quietude and thoughtfulness. Together, these set a cultural scene where important matters are addressed, where people's needs and desires can be serviced, where well-being is cultivated, where proper conduct is respected.

Allowing time for thought is necessary for many practical and social matters, as when an employee is offered a new job opportunity. Mika described a work situation where an employee was offered new tasks. The boss suggested he take time to reflect carefully what he thought about this. The employer did not want the employee to make a hasty decision, but to weigh the issues carefully and from different angles. As Mika put it: "It is crucial to take your time and think about things."

Being alone in a good way, then, gives one time to think carefully, to formulate one's thoughts, to focus and reflect. Given such time, one is indeed permitted to reflect about things, to think carefully, to ponder matters. In the process, there is the social creation of more freedom for the person for thinking, for being alone in her or his thoughts. This is a crucial part of decision-making processes. In fact, it is an essential means toward making good decisions. In the process, it offers a means of respecting others; giving them the proper time; getting their input, investment, and involvement. This enhances the quality of subsequent social actions, creating better instrumental and social outcomes.

A NATURAL WEB OF FINNISHNESS

A "natural way of being" as discussed here is linked to many features of Finnish interpersonal life. One important interactional feature of many social situations is "pidättyväinen" (holding yourself in, being properly reserved). This is at times a laudable interactional objective, that is, to be properly quiet and reserved while being silently attentive to others. Those whose activities are not conducted in this way may be identified as "erottuvat" (as sticking out or as inappropriately standing out). This latter quality is less laudable and has often been mentioned by Finnish friends as something "Americans tend to do." Not surprisingly, some Finnish viewers saw Safer as this when walking down the Finnish street with his "American face" on or when he "laughed too much" (on line 330). One way of acting according to this natural way—that is, as "holding oneself in," and not "sticking out"—is to be "varautunut" (properly on your guard) or "tarkkailevainen" (properly observant). If one is interested in speaking with another, this is the kind of cultural action that should precede that talk—that is, one should be, as Koriseva described, guarded and observant before approaching another to speak to them. All of this, being properly reserved, quiet, on your guard, and observant, can take place if one is "quiet in a good way." In social life conducted this way, so much can, and should, go without saying!

If the social occasion was deemed appropriate for speaking, what would one do? If one's watchful eye noticed a proper moment for speaking and guessed another is perhaps socially available for interaction, it is best "before I pick up the nerve to come and talk to you" [ennen kuin uskaltaudumme] to think through what one wants to say carefully prior to speaking. Then, if speaking to another still seems possible and permissible, one should do so, especially in educational settings, in a proper "asiallinen" style, that is, in a style that is straight, short, and to the point (see Carbaugh, 2005; Wilkins, 2005).

One male Finn's website played with these features of "matter-of-fact" talk in this direct, humorous way:

> Communication in Finland can be described in one sentence, if you've got nothing to say: shut up. If you, on the other hand, have something to say, say it straight, brutal but truthful, whatever it is. Don't try any slick small talk. Again the Finnish culture shows not only its elegance but also its efficiency, wordless communication is, in fact, always the most truthful.

In a comment like this, one can hear several premises in a Finnish code: Speak only if you have something to say; when speaking, be direct, truthful, and to the point; do not force others to engage in unnecessary talk such as "slick small talk"; much can and should be said without words. Knowing what is being said without words and how to interpret this in a good way are essential to understanding this natural way of being.

A FINNISH COMMUNICATION CODE

On line 190, Safer alludes to an unwritten Finnish "code." Here we take that folk idea and use it in a technical sense in order to formulate systematically a Finnish "natural way of being." Being "olla omissa oloissaan" in a "natural way" is, of course, a social accomplishment, something one can and must get done with the cooperation of others. As such, it is an achievement in social contexts. In other words, in order to effectively do this, one must indicate that one is so being to others, and one needs to be able to identify others who are so being; and this, according to the code, should be respected. This way of being is, then, a mode and form of social action and must, as such, in some ways invoke and at times creatively play with a known code that renders such actions coherent, efficacious, and valuable. This is the kind of code Knutas and Koriseva were echoing with their words, Heikki was presuming on the train, parents may invoke when coming home from work, and Finnish people presumably need at times for a sense of well-being and development; this also is the kind of code that Tiina sorely missed when she was in the family car driving across the Iowan countryside.

What are elements in this code? What cultural premises enable the social noticing and the effective acting of this "natural" way? Here we turn to a more formal explication of that code, always individually applied and context dependent, organized around its central defining premises:

> Social and interpersonal life includes, periodically, quiet moments.
> There is a basic want or desire in people occasionally to be uninterrupted or quiet.
> These moments and this want are natural and normal.
> These moments can be produced alone (as isolated actions) or with others (as social events).
> These moments can be produced in various social scenes, both public and private.
> These moments can involve various possible acts such as peaceful reflection, deep concentration, or creative contemplation, but can also be simple moments of relaxation.
> These moments are linked to privacy, through reserve, which is to be respected.
> These moments enable a sense of peaceful well-being and allow for one's development.
> These moments protect one (and others) from impositions and intrusions.
> Speaking with others is a potential threat to these moments and this want.

Note how the premises summarized here set the stage for a kind of communicative action that has cultural integrity. The stage, so set, is part of a cultural script for proper conduct, itself an unspoken understanding, providing a taken-for-granted feature of unspoken social life (cf. Goddard and Wierzbicka, 2004). In the process, when there is quietude, something important is transpiring, and this should be respected, for people want and deserve protection from unwanted intrusion. All of this can play upon a socially enacted stage of silent activity. On this stage, and because it can, on occasion, be set in this way, speaking enters with a particular force, not as filling a silence, not as a presence within an absence, but potentially as a breach, cracking the valuable code of quietude among those present.

I shall never forget my first bus ride in Finland, late one November night, when I sat in the front seat initiating a conversation with a person across the aisle from me. I thought we were more or less alone on the bus. As I began speaking, however, I felt like I had intruded and was astonished to discover the bus itself was full, with me being the sole speaker! Such cooperative, socially produced quietude had escaped my notice!

A Finnish cultural scene can be set, then, with quietude as its primary mode, silence as its structuring norm, people being directly and knowingly engaged in this as an efficacious action. When so set, speaking can enter as an intrusion. Of course, not all Finnish scenes are set this way, nor is this quietude always valued.

Yet, when it is, when people are being undisturbed together and thinking, important messages are activated about the communicative event, the proper acts that compose it, the proper places for quietude and speaking, and the relation of the one to the other.

Scenes and moments such as these create a prominent social position for participants, as ones who are thoughtfully engaged in their own thoughts and should not be disturbed. Planning for actions of "olla omissa oloissaan" and "mietiskellä" and living them set the stage for this social position, and its interactional deployment. This is a way of structuring social relations for the moment at least as properly distant, one from another, protecting each other's space, yet engaged together in a moment of solidarity in silence. Such moments are desirable, and in fact should be created periodically in various social institutions from the family to education and are most important when people need peaceful reflection, time to reflect or relax or engage in careful thought.

Cultural moments and wants like these provide a distinctive form for, and thus are linked to, Finnish conceptions of the person. In short, one should speak only when one is not intruding and when one has something to say that is worthy of another's consideration. Otherwise, one should defer to others by being a quiet, respectful, and verbally reserved person. Being in this natural way is to be one who can and should watch and listen, rather than one who is engaged in needless chatter. The motives for acting in this way are thus based in a deep appreciation of quietude and the basic human want of a person to be undisturbed or unimpeded. For this to be effectively practiced, a social scene must be so understood and motivated. "Olla omissa oloissaan" and "mietiskellä" provide the terms for such moments and express the motives for a "natural" way of acting. In this sense, these moments illustrate not only a personal desire, but moreover, cultural motives for moments of action.

Aspects of this Finnish version of personhood have been discussed by analysts and historians of Finnish culture. The epigraphs at the beginning of the paper by Markku Koivusalo illustrate the importance in Finnish discourse of being alone and quietness, linking these explicitly to considerateness and strength in character as well as enduring social relationships. These qualities are active, as Koivusalo says, in "shared unspoken gestures," not "by exchanged words." Knowing what is getting said without words, and its importance, is crucial for this aspect of Finnish character, indeed, to be itself. In fact, it is one defining feature of Finnishness.

The Finnish historian Matti Klinge (1990) has discussed how "the Nordic self" is at home on the periphery of Europe, in its beautiful northern hinterlands. Here, Finnish character has been forged while being exposed to nature's extreme demands of cold, enduring darkness (in winter) and warmer, ever-present light (in summer). Withstanding this wide range of conditions both requires and creates a strength of character, an appreciation of simplicity, demanding that one require no more than is needed, while appreciating nature's emphatically diverse offerings.

In such circumstances, and even amidst Finland's unmatched technologies of today, one typically texts rather than talks, one appreciates and values how to "go it alone," to be observant of one's world and others in it, to get things done without too much fuss or without demanding more than is required from oneself or others. The ever-watchful eye of Finnishness is honed in such a geographic and cultural scene, quietly observing the world express itself, alone, with others, and knowing what to do as a result (see Koivusalo, 1999, p. 49).

Over time, there have been diverse political seasons, like winter and summer, that have forged Finland between different circumstances. From the Middle Ages until 1808–1809, Finland was occupied by the West, as an integral part of the kingdom of Sweden. Swedish appointments of bishops and the Swedish language itself put Finland, Finns, and the Finnish language in a minority position. As such, it was prudent to be vigilantly attentive to others, especially to non-Finns and what they thought of Finns, as not only a routine occupation, but indeed a necessity for a continuing, productive social and political life. Similarly, a semi-autonomous Finland was part of Russia from 1809 until 1917, when a similar stance was advisable. A clear, enduring sense is maintained to this day that Finnish life is something other than that of these Swedish, or Russian, or in this case American others.

Although during these earlier eras Swedish culture and language infiltrated Finnish life, Russian language and culture did not. As a result of these dynamics, Finnishness is seen as something different from the surrounding others, yet deeply concerned and preoccupied with what the others think of it. Finnishness has thus been conceived historically in negative terms as NOT Russian or NOT talkative. Finnish life is felt relative to these others, yet as dependent on neither; thus the famous Finnish saying: "Swedes no more; Never Russians; Let us be Finns." It is noteworthy that the latter period of Russian rule saw the flowering of the Finnish language and a budding cultivation of a distinctive Finnishness in literature, music, and character. Finnish language and democracy developed to the point of passing laws that allowed all women to vote (second in the world) and even be elected to the Finnish parliament (first in the world). A Finnish sense of group life, as all cultural features for acting and general ways of so being, has therefore derived from various historical, geographic, and political circumstances.

Yet, even if hard wired to the Finnish cultural and political landscape, the qualities of Finnishness discussed here are not in any deterministic way linked to any one person. In other words, Finnishness as discussed here is a property of Finnish social practices, not necessarily housed within any one individual or context. When speaking on these matters I am often asked if Finns are indeed this way. My response is this: when "olla omissa oloissaan" or "mietiskellä," these qualities are indeed active, and they are felt as "luonteva tapa olla" (see Berry, 2011). I do not know what is inside any one Finnish person. Some like doing this more than others. Some occasions call for it more than others. So, I do think the Finnish practices of concern in this report are cultural practices that presume and create some sense of Finnishness discussed earlier. In this sense, Finnishness lives in the world of Finnish practices. No one, in Finland or elsewhere, is required to perform any one of these practices. However, when in Finland, there are times when some so act. And it is this action, its cultural shape and meanings, that has held our attention here.

In order to grapple with that world of coded conduct, the one puzzling to US viewers, Safer, and Schultz, we have examined a small set of Finnish terms for those practices; observed events made relevant through those terms; interpreted some of the meanings about communication, social relations, and persons presumed for those terms; and for those practices. In this way, we have come to some understanding of a Finnish "natural way of being." Living in this way can provide for some Finns coveted moments of "being alone in a good way." These provide bases for Finnish conduct, illustrating a Finnish code for so being. These, of course, are not the only practices of Finnishness in Finnish society, nor are these the only features of this particular practice. These terms, acts, events, and premises are, however, central to a part of Finnishness, and this provides basic elements in a Finnish cultural discourse, a few trees in a rich Finnish forest, something akin to a traditional memorial tree, providing seeds for proper and further Finnish growth, cultivating cultural activities in a Finnish clearing, to be seen, thoughtfully and peacefully enacted, yet not necessarily heard.

NOTES

1 The studies reported here have cited and used as part of their analytic strategy a particular theoretical framework for investigating meta-communication practices (Carbaugh, 1989, 2017a). That framework was based upon careful cross-cultural study of fifty such terms in seventeen cultural communities. Since its publication, several research reports have used, among other investigative tools, this investigative framework (e.g., Baxter, 1993; Baxter and Goldsmith, 1990; Bloch, 2003; Carbaugh, 1999; Fitch, 1998; Garrett, 1993; Hall and Noguchi, 1995; Hall and Valde, 1995; Katriel, 2004; Sawyer, 2004; Wilkins, 2005). This program of work has now explored over 100 such practices in several different languages, including American Sign Language, Chinese, Danish, English, Finnish, German, Hebrew, Japanese, Russian, and Spanish (see the chapters in Carbaugh, 2017b).

2 The investigative framework, in short, draws attention to two kinds of meta-communicative phenomena: 1) cultural terms used to identify communicative action and 2) the communicative actions referenced and related to those terms. Descriptive elements in the framework draw special attention to the variety of uses of such terms in conversation, as well as the variety of actions potentially being identified, including communicative acts, events, and/or styles. These form the descriptive bases of the accounts. The additional value in exploring these phenomena is the unveiling of rich meanings, literally and symbolically, that these terms and enactments make salient. The second set of elements in the framework explore these, the interpretive elements, structuring explorations of the deep significance, the ethos and ideology at play, drawing attention to the meanings participants are making

through these terms and actions. These include the meanings literally about communication itself (especially its modes, structuring norms, tone, and efficaciousness) and those that are more metaphorically about sociality (social positions, social relationships, social institutions) and personhood (beliefs about persons, loci of motives, sites of consciousness, links to history). This is the framework at use in the preceding as well as the following analyses.

3   Such studies contribute to other related programs of research such as Aakhus' on "process" (2001), Nelson's on "conflict" (2001), and Huspek and Kendall's on "shit talk" (1991). Each, like the aforementioned works, draws attention to native categories for communication and the social practices these make relevant. Fieldwork for the ethnographic study reported later began in November 1992 and is ongoing today. Most of the fieldwork occurred in the Häme, middle Lake region of Finland to the north of Helsinki. Some Finnish commentators, those from within the Häme region and those outside of it, have called this region, "the really Finnish part of Finland." Data consist of segments from field observations, interviews, surveys, video documents, and various other materials in which activities are identified by Finns as "a natural way to be." The primary corpus consists of several hundred instances of such terms (discussed later) as well as observations of the activities so identified. Analyses proceeded through the framework discussed earlier in three phases of descriptive research: transcribing segments in which such terms are being used, verbal accounts of the terms being used, and observations of activities so identified. This descriptive phase was complemented by three phases of interpretive analyses focused on the literal meanings such terms, accounts, and observations make about communication itself and the more metaphorical meanings being expressed about sociality and personhood. The descriptive and interpretive analyses together, then, generate basic elements in an ethnographic account of communication, with the account demonstrating how communication is being practiced and coded from a Finnish perspective. The code is summarized later in the chapter.

4   Like Safer, I (DC) am a native speaker of English. Unlike Safer, I have lived in Finland and speak a little bit of Finnish. Yet, I am admittedly an outsider, and while Finnish custom attends carefully to what outsiders think about Finland, the deck is stacked against me when it comes to speaking about such matters, for I cannot speak as a genuine Finn or in fluent Finnish about Finnish things. Nonetheless, I can try to participate in the conversation about such things, will endeavor to do so productively, and offer my efforts in the spirit of developing a shared understanding of such things. Just as outsiders to America, Frenchmen Alexis de Tocqueville and Herve Varenne, have offered most telling insights about American culture, others can sometimes offer an interesting reading of insiders' concerns.

5   The cluster of Finnish terms identified here are largely part of an unspoken code that is presumed and valued. When spoken, the task can be to question this very presumption and value, and thus turn matters into a negative, thereby alleging or identifying their absence.

6   A detailed analysis and rationale for the concept of quietude appears in Berry, Nurmikari-Berry, and Carbaugh (2004).

Chapter 7

Reporting Cultures
Moving from a Mirror to a Window

In the prior chapters we have focused on ways a popular US American discourse has cast Finns as "inexpressive," "shy," and "sad." We have noted how these verbal interpretations derive from popular features of a US American discourse that say one should be "open," "outgoing," and "happy."[1] We demonstrated how the quality of "inexpressiveness" (in short) does not say anything necessarily from a Finnish perspective about Finns through a Finnish discourse. From a Finnish stance, "thoughtfulness, privacy, and respect" are seen and hearable as socially situated values and as momentarily valuable. The play between these discourses, as summarized here, demonstrates how the process of seeing and speaking about a cultural other can get caught within either discourse—by "mirroring" its own contrasting features—even as it believes it is saying something important about another.

To elaborate the point a bit, we have used many features of the "Tango Finlandia" broadcast to demonstrate this point and process. We have focused on the verbal interpretations of Finns in everyday English as "shy" and "sad." Both of these terms contrast with US American discursive values of being extroverted and happy. The attribution of "shy" and "sad" thus gives voice to another but does so within a US discourse through a kind of contrasting negation, contrasting with expressiveness and negating the resounding themes of openness and happiness so prominent in American popular discourse. In other words, saying "they are shy and sad" contrasts with this, and again, the point mirrors a system of meaning activated in popular American uses of English.

There is, however, as we have analyzed previously, a window into another world, a different Finnish source of meanings about these matters. From this view, the same "sounds and images"—which US Americans see as "shy" and "sad"—are heard to echo different primary Finnish texts, serious Finnish actions and premises of "holding yourself in properly," acknowledging the productive value of "melancholy," privacy, and the related values of "respect" and "quietude." Being shy and sad are largely irrelevant in this Finnish discursive terrain, as these verbal interpretations are echoing a different primary source, the indigenous sounds of a Finnish "natural way of being." From this view, "we are a respectful people"; in some social times, we deem it good to be quiet. This Finnish source is, of course, inactive and largely unknown to other English speakers or non-Finnish viewers.

US viewers puzzle long and hard over the Finnish idea that one does not have to say "I love you" a lot. From a US American discourse that embraces "sharing feelings," a Finnish account of "not saying I love you" can seem counterintuitive, contrasting with and negating this value in "sharing your feelings" (see Carbaugh, 1988). In Finnish, however, there is a different cultural bedrock and reality underlying the performance. It presumes several things in some public scenes: One should not say things that are obvious. If one says such an obvious thing to one who is obviously loved, and this is knowingly obvious to the other, then it sounds suspiciously redundant (or even silly), perhaps even drawing the statement itself into question (Carbaugh, 2005). The various features in the video text thus are seen and heard from the vantage of different cultural discourses.

In this chapter, we make the intercultural process we are describing here as explicit as possible. We do so by explicating the process rather schematically, by formulating seven principles that serve to describe how this process not only typically works, but can be moved further in productive directions that will increase critical intercultural understanding. We feel some such process must be at the heart of a more robust intercultural competence, for journalists and laypeople alike, as we dwell within increasingly multicultural worlds and global societies.

CULTURAL REPORTING: FROM A NAÏVE MIRROR TO A CRITICAL CONVERSATION THROUGH DIFFERENT CODES

As we explored the dynamics described earlier, among others, we have come to understand how a complex process of seeing and speaking about cultural others involves fundamentally a seeing and speaking about ourselves. As we discussed in our first chapter, we have been focusing our analyses upon four everyday genres of communication, including a "news program," everyday reports about the news, talking about culturally different others, and characterizing our own cultural selves. We have explored these genres in two languages, Finnish and English, with special attention to cultural terms for communicative action, comparing and contrasting parts of each. Our analyses have given shape to two popular cultural discourses and two codes, noticing that each is active in an echoing sequence within the text, but the dialogic echoes come from two directions: one from one's native language, the other from one's non-native language. For this reason, when developing understanding across languages and cultures, these are best understood more deeply as parallel voices, as distinct ways of seeing and speaking, by attending carefully to focal images, potent phrases, and the variety of meanings in each. We have identified these discursive dynamics in order to unveil two cultural discourses in, about, and through these everyday genres.

We summarize this complex intercultural process of seeing and speaking here simply at first, through a roughly linear, but also importantly cyclical form. Our summary moves from a description of the dynamics we have studied (especially in phase 1) to a more critical stance, as it proposes a process for moving reports as these, especially news reports, into a better intercultural or third space.[2]

In a nutshell, we discuss the process in seven stages and punctuate it in the beginning with an initial encounter or viewing of a difference. We illustrate the process here with examples of a US American reporter about Finland (as US) and as a Finnish reporter about the United States (as Finn):

1) Notice and speak about the other as a contrast with self (as in news reports) (e.g., US: Finns are inexpressive, shy, and sad; Finn: Americans are superficial and unnecessarily talkative).
2) Notice the expressed contrast is based in a negation of your code (e.g., US: being sad and shy negates being outgoing and happy; Finn: being talkative negates being reserved and thoughtful).
3) Notice the contrast and negation does not necessarily say anything important about the Other (e.g., US: we say they value being inexpressive and shy: do they say that?; Finn: we say they are superficial: do they say that?)
4) Note how the contrast and negation often lead to a negative evaluation of other because "they" allegedly negate valued parts of your own discourse (e.g., both: what we do not value, or believe, they do).
5) Explore the other's discourse from their view (through their language, communication practices, and culture) (e.g., notice what they say: US, we are friendly; Finns, we are respectful and thoughtful).
6) Re-view your discourse from the view of the other's discourse (e.g., Finnish discourse says about US: You are disrespectful and superficial, what might this reveal about popular US-ness?; US discourse says about Finns: You are shy and silent, what might this say about popular Finnish-ness?).
7) Goal: Converse through enriched comparative discourses of self and other.

One of our observations and one of our most humble findings is that most discourses we have seen operate solely within the contrastive form of phase 1. In other words, we have noticed on most occasions when people are viewing and verbalizing about culturally different others, journalists and viewers alike, they are speaking within the frame of their cultural discourse, thus mirroring more about their cultural self than they are about the others. This contrastive form of discourse largely defeats its goal of understanding another.

Using our principles further, we find, in effect, that the contrastive discourse accomplishes 1–4, but does so in a way largely unaware of the processes summarized in 2–4. Making them explicit, however, helps move our perspective into a critical space.

Some of the most unproductive forms of inter-religious, interracial or inter-ethnic stereotyping are stuck in phase 1, unknowingly accomplishing the dynamics of negation and negative judgments about culturally different others (cf. Bailey, 2000; Chick, 1990; Covarrubias, 2008; Scollon and Scollon, 1990; Tannen, 1986). Implementing the subsequent "moves"—through education and training—will help extend insights into forms of reporting about others, from everyday acts of reporting culture, to newer interactional forms that explicitly engage intercultural or multicultural matters. We have worked with them, for example, to enrich forms of interfaith dialogue, dynamics between languages, and intercultural dialogue more generally.

But first, why is it so common we get stuck within a communication form that sees and speaks, or in technical terms, codes the other through features that contrast with our own? Again, why? Because the terms, phrases, images, norms, and meanings people typically employ are of one and only one cultural discourse, and it is the tendency of a discourse to perpetuate itself, its concepts, beliefs, and values. As noted throughout this book, this means that our selection of items to discuss and debate about others are more products of our own discursive frame than they are, in any sense, of another. As a consequence, our discourse about another may react to that other, but it is not typically *of* another. This dynamic is one we must understand better as educators, journalists, mediators, lawyers, doctors, and citizens in a multicultural and global society. (It would help us in the political arena as well.)

Once we more ably notice, then hopefully better understand, these initial and asynchronous parts of this intercultural process, we can move more productively onward—to what we discuss in phases 5–7—to better engage others based in ways they recognize as their own, then critically reflecting upon what we recognize as our own. If we are able to do that together, and it is a very difficult task indeed, we can move forward with more deeply informed practices of communication. Others have discussed such a process somewhat similarly (e.g., Bailey, 2000; Chick, 1990; Covarrubias, 2008; Dallmayr, 1996, esp. pp. 1–62; Eades, 2006; see especially Wilkins, 2007). What we contribute is a location of the process in actual cultural discourses, its demonstration in a deep mass mediated process, its extensive grounding in everyday genres of social life, and its theoretical treatment as situated communication practices, all aimed toward a culturally informed discursive mediation through educational and dialogic means.

We will formulate this process in a more detailed way through our seven principles.

PRINCIPLES ONE AND TWO: ASYNCHRONOUS DIFFERENCE, CONTRAST, AND NEGATION

For decades we have heard comments about others in the form: they are not us. We have discussed elsewhere how people engage sensitive cultural issues across languages and cultural fields (see Berry, Carbaugh, Innrater-Moser, Nurmikari-Berry, and Oesch, 2008). In doing so, we identify the "not us" based upon our own ideas and values, as when they are not happy, not expressive, and do not say "I love you"! The earlier chapters provide ample illustration of this discursive contrasting of other as not-self, both in journalism and in everyday life.

We could summarize this feature of this discourse more abstractly with a proposition about it: when communicating about cultural others, we use our own premises about persons, emotions, and actions, thereby noticing first what contrasts with those premises, essentially saying, they are not us. This impression of not-us is a verbal characterization of an other all the while being formulated through our own discourse of who we are. What results is a discourse that contrasts those people, their actions and emotions, and their world with our own by casting them as a negative reflection of us.

The specific discursive dynamics we have discussed earlier are difficult to capture in a simple way. We have, however, tried to formulate some of them with the two principles of contrast—there is a presumed difference that leads us to notice and negation—that difference is something we are not. This play of contrasts involves the rather unknowing discursive use of one's own cultural premises about persons and practices and their negation in an effort to comprehend a different other.

Consider some specific instances of this contrasting dynamic. The American discourse noted earlier identifies Finns as "inexpressive." Why? This quality has become relevant for understanding Finns precisely because it contrasts with a cultural premise held dear to so many Americans. That is the norm that one should be expressive, open, and talkative. In other words, based upon the premise that US Americans are (and should be verbally) expressive, US Americans assess Finns as being not that, as being in-expressive, and further presumes that they value that so-called by Americans "inexpressiveness"! This is but one example of the contrastive feature of this discourse, of how identifying another treats the cultural other as not one-self and attributing that anti-feature as a value, in being that other-than-us way.

Note, then, further, that the quality of "inexpressiveness" attributed to Finns in this discourse is relevant only because it contrasts with a US American premise that values expressiveness, or being honest, or expressing yourself (Carbaugh,

1988). The noticing is itself a negative reflection of one's cultural self. This, of course, does not mean that this type of "inexpressiveness"—in its US American discursive sense—is at all relevant to understanding a Finnish sense of Finnishness, at least as it is spoken and seen in this video-text. In other words, this echo of the American voice is not hearable from the Finnish one, even if the "inexpressiveness" attributed to Finns is being understood by Americans in that way. "Inexpressiveness" in this US sense does not express the Finnish sense of "being alone in a natural way."

What this US discourse of "inexpressiveness" of Finns does mean is caught solely within a US American value of expressiveness, thereby saying more about this US value (and its contrasts with negations) and much less about anything like it elsewhere, most notably in Finland. The same holds true for the alleged sadness and shyness being attributed to Finns, for each points to dimensions whose meanings counter the US American values of being happy and extroverted and say nothing necessarily from a Finnish view. This is the play of asynchrony in actions and meanings of phases 1–2.[3]

PRINCIPLES THREE AND FOUR: EVALUATING OTHER, INVERTING SELF

The contrasting and negative properties of this discourse set the stage for subsequent dimensions of this process. These involve an inversion in which the other's difference is evaluated as a deficit, that deficit is cast as a value of the other, the other thus being made a deficient version of one's proper cultural self. In this way, one's own senses of belief and value are inverted to make sense of "theirs," with the difference giving way, typically, to an evaluation of that different other as a deficient other.[4]

So, with this US discourse, it is not simply that Finns, by contrast with "expressiveness," are deemed "inexpressive," but moreover that so-called "inexpressiveness" can be turned into a positive value of Finnishness. The impression the US American cultural discourse creates, then, is not only that Finns contrast with Americans, but also through the contrasts a reversal occurs; the subsequent meanings are negations of positive US qualities—being inexpressive, sad, and shy, and these are turned rather remarkably into Finnish values! The belief is easily formulated within this US discourse, for it counters its dominant culture and is parasitic upon it: the other actually values being inexpressive, sad, and shy! This is the work of a rhetoric of astonishment. Amazingly, through contrast, negation, and a cultural discursive inversion, what we consider a deficiency is turned into their virtue! The cumulative effect creates the discursive themes of a puzzle and of astonishment discussed in Chapter 3.

At the base of these dynamics are sacred beliefs and values from the vantage point of the respective cultural discourses. In short, the one dominant US American cultural discourse reflects and creates in its use specific beliefs and values, in this case about openness, happiness, and extroversion. The discourse presumes and highlights these features as relevant and valued, the basic beliefs being that people can and should "be open" about themselves to others, be happy, and talk with others if at all possible. When used, the discourse creates the feeling not only that they—as inexpressive, sad, and shy—are different from us, in being "what we are not," but moreover that "we—as talkative, happy, and extroverted—are different from them, being what they are not." The discourse creates boundaries of meanings along limited (and limiting) dimensions, which differentiate in both directions. By focusing on them (as a topic) we can say that they are not only different, but identify that difference as directly opposite of us, and in so doing affirm all at once who we are, who we are not, and what they are and are not. The discourse thus grounds, and is indeed grounded upon, a cultural model for a US self and its cultural premises of belief and value, as it ultimately fails to grasp another.

These premises also unknowingly ground an evaluative sense of the contrasts, so it is not simply that they do what we don't value (e.g., at times be silent and sad), but they actually value what we don't do (e.g., being silent and sad). This dynamic goes both ways. What each claims as a deficiency, shyness to US Americans or "unnecessary talkativeness" to Finns, is a value to the other! The discourse thus moves along dimensions of contrasts, from noticing a difference, to its negation of something of value to you, to the others' valuing this negation, and thus to its identification as a deficient quality in the other. As the discourse depicts a cultural other in this way, it thus deeply implicates its own sense of its self. This complex dynamic is again what we call earlier a rhetoric of astonishment, as it is at play in this televised and many other communicative scenes.

The eventual effect of this rhetoric is a discursive illusion of otherness—illusory because one's own discourse, like its speakers, has not left its cultural home or entered into the discourse and dimensions the premises and parameters of the other. Trapped in its webs of signification, as Geertz (1973) has put it, in terms of its dimensions, one's discourse has not penetrated and has thus muted the meanings of those culturally different others. As Geertz says further, our goal as cultural interpreters is to hear others and converse with them. To this point, we have not heard them or conversed with them. We have only spoken directly and indirectly of ourselves.

As the discourse of astonishment makes sense of an other by mirroring its own terms, it does not necessarily say anything salient about the other in their own terms on the basis of their practices and premises. If productively investigative of the matter, by entering a door or window into another world, we can eventually find that they have other dimensions and parameters of belief and judgment about themselves (not just reflections of our own). We can find the others are not what we say they are, for what we say reflects more who we are than who they are. And, of course, the dynamic works in both directions.

Our discussion of the principles up to this point has focused primarily on the US American discourse as its illustrative case. The same general principles of these discursive dynamics apply also to the Finnish discourse. For example, one of the criticisms Finnish viewers made repeatedly about the scenes in "Tango Finlandia" and the Americans participating in them, as well as elsewhere, was, "they're so superficial" (or in Finnish, "pinnallinen"). In Finland and Northern Europe generally, one often hears the claim, "Americans are superficial." In fact, early in my field studies, I was asked by a Finnish scholar if I could please explain why Americans are "so superficial" (with my reply in Carbaugh, 2005). The presumption itself reflects a system of Finnish premises about the Finnish cultural self, with these being applied in order to evaluate "Americans" as such. Why is this so? Finns can be expected to value and to act on the basis of "hiljaisuus" (a positive silent, reserve), "pidättyväisyys" (tactful respect and control of one's emotions), and "olla omissa oloissaan" (privacy in one's own space and honoring the privacy of others in social situations). On the basis of these Finnish terms, practices, and premises, those who are talkative, too easily expressive of their feelings, and intrusively verbal can quickly seem, based upon their taken-for-granted discourse, not properly reserved, in control, or thoughtful. In sum, they are rather "pinnallinen," or superficial.

The Finnish conclusion, then, that Americans are "superficial" is built upon these and other Finnish premises, dimensions, and rules. In terms of the Finnish discourse presented in Chapter 6, Finns can at times expressively value being quiet, thoughtful, and private. As a result, when dealing with US Americans, specific Finnish dimensions of contrast are activated and inverted, making discursive sense of Americans as overly talkative, a bit thoughtless at times, and all too quick to fill quiet moments by publicizing their feelings verbally, or by producing what Finns have called a lot of "unnecessary talk." In fact, these qualities, which contrast with Finnish premises, are often applied to American television as well, as when American commentators produce telecommunications that are—as was said by Finns about "Tango Finlandia"—one sided, misleading, mistaken, rushed, and put together too quickly. Such texts clearly deny the properly silent, presumably distant, thoughtful, deep reserve the Finnish discourse can claim for itself and through which would be provided a better, albeit Finnish, communication.

These are the particular, abstract, and general principles of contrast, negation, inversion, and evaluation operating in this intercultural discourse. In summary, the principle of contrast goes like this. On the basis of visual scenes and verbalizations about an other, notice features that contrast most vividly with what is familiar to you. By focusing on these scenes and words, one unknowingly activates and eventually reveals one's own semantic dimensions of contrast between self and other (e.g., inexpressive-expressive, sad-happy, shy-extroverted). In the process, what is highlighted about the other as different from you is a negative shadow of your discourse about your cultural self, thereby identifying features allegedly in the other that are unlike your self. These dimensions—of contrast and negation—consist of continua, of more and less of something, with the poles that counter the self being attributed—through the process of inversion—to the other. And those counter poles, when inverted, become cast as values of the other. These discursive poles of countering your culture, in the process, are deemed apt and appropriate virtues of the other, even though they derive from one's own cultural discourse and do not necessarily say anything that is salient from the other's view through their terms and dimensions (e.g., as quiet, thoughtful, and private).

This is the way intercultural discourse can play out, sometimes in a seemingly interminable way. Yet how does one move beyond this? Where does one go from here?

PRINCIPLES FIVE AND SIX, OPENING A WINDOW TO ANOTHER CULTURAL DISCOURSE: EXPLORATION AND FURTHER CRITICAL REFLECTION

We have introduced this movement earlier and yet find it to be most difficult; it requires, to some degree, relinquishing the central hold one's discourse has upon one's own sensibilities. For example, especially with the US Constitution and the outpouring of "happiness studies," how can one possibly question the "pursuit of happiness" as a central goal in social life? With expressiveness linked immediately to political value in "free speech," why should one not be verbally expressive? How can one entertain the idea that another goal may be equally valued and at times maybe even more valued and valuable? If one has been raised in a family and society that encourages you to speak your mind—or exclaims, express yourself!—what good can there be in remaining silent, in not speaking, in asking others to speak for yourself? Moving beyond the comfort and boundaries of one's sensibilities can, of course be difficult, if not at times impossible.

The difficulty is pronounced in at least two directions. One can involve confronting a difference of a large degree of magnitude that seems almost too great to fathom, as when a butcher of beef is told cows are sacred animals. Another is a difficulty in its subtlety as when one is told the important nonverbal expressions are located more in the eyes and brows than in the face more generally. In the first, we are fish out of water; in the second, we're not sure in which water we are swimming. Understanding each involves a complex process of recognizing the limits of one's own discourse so one can grasp features of another. This includes understanding not only one's own discourse and its dimensions, but the terms of another discourse and its dimensions of meaning.

In the research we report in this book, we have moved in this way beyond the boundaries of one cultural discourse by introducing to US American viewers features of the Finnish language, some routines of Finnish social life, specific acts and events of Finnish communication. In so doing, following Finnish viewers, we have rendered some of the cultural sense and significance of each to Finnish people themselves. We note that many but, of course, not all Finnish viewers had some sense of a US American discourse, of spoken English, and of routines in American lives. It is this sort of education in alternative cultural discourses that allows, when successful—and this is not always successful!—a transformative move within and beyond the terms of one's discourse.[5]

Some examples of this productively transformative process are evident in some US American viewers' reactions when a door was opened to a Finnish discourse:

> It never occurred to me before that saying "I love you" could be understood that way. The Finns have a point. Why do we continually say something that is obvious?

Or on a different topic:

> This whole "be happy" thing is interesting. I had never questioned that. I always thought I should be happy. But when you think about it, you can't be happy all the time, and you probably shouldn't even try to be. There are good reasons and times when you should feel other things.

By introducing some different language, based upon translations across cultures of Finnish ideas, such as "being thoughtful" and "spending good time in silence" and the virtues of "melancholy" or "sadness," some US American viewers were opened to different possibilities in human understanding and action. This is the dynamic we describe here as "moving beyond one's discourse." This is largely an educational process where one begins seeing things in a different way and is given deeper cultural resources for understanding the difference in a productive way. The point is not simply that things are different, although that is truly the case, but that the difference is deep and can be known to some degree as based in different discursive customs and traditions. Knowing this lays a base for an enhanced understanding, even if not agreement.

One means we have used toward this end involves viewers rescripting parts of the broadcast as they think their own cultural representative (e.g., Knutas for Finns) or the other (e.g., Safer for Americans) sees and speaks in it. For example, after hearing Finnish viewers' comments about the broadcast, we asked US American viewers to paraphrase Knutas' comments in an effort to capture the Finnish meanings in them. They would give these comments to Finnish viewers in an effort to test their fledgling ability to understand and use features of the Finnish discourse. Reactions from the Finnish viewers were then instructive and useful to enhance the US American viewers' understandings of the Finnish discourse.

But moreover, by the end, the exercise helped US American viewers critically reflect upon their own presumptions, premises, and meanings. This exercise with viewers from various cultural stances has proven not easy, but productive of better intercultural understanding and the processes of building it. Critical distance was created from one's own discourse just as less distance was created to another (Carbaugh, 1989/1990).

Beyond our focal case of "Tango Finlandia," our pedagogical door opens here to all other worlds, including religious differences—for example, between Islam and Christianity, political differences between bipartisan and alliance democracies or between autocratic and parliamentary rule, economic differences between capitalism and socialism, and so on. All education to some degree is necessarily caught in the process as described here, yet when transcending the limits of one's discourse, the teaching moment can become exceptional, as one faces the relatively unilateral and blind assertion of one's own ways or, as we move onward here, toward an understanding of multiple cultures and a dialogic engagement among them. To get there, we must develop the competence to critically reflect from whence we, and others, speak (and see, feel, sense our worlds).[6]

REFLECTING UPON CULTURAL DISCOURSES AS A MOVE TOWARD CRITICAL PLURALISM

There are several particular challenges that watching "Tango Finlandia" can present to US American viewers. At first, how could one possibly positively value "being shy"? Yet, as things move along, what if the "difficulty making social contact" expressed by Safer is actually something else, a proper reserve, a respect of distance between people, a value in people having their own time alone to sit and think. And if this is a deep collective value—that is, at least on some occasions— then what does this say about a propensity at times to want or even to demand social (verbal) contact from others? Where does that leave this expressed value?

This kind of questioning introduces the value of an explicit comparative analysis among cultural discourses, a critical pluralism. Although discomforting at times, this kind of questioning can create benefits in at least two directions: it can create a careful critical assessment of one's own discourse; it can also come to some better understanding of another; both aspects can develop together.

Consider the following comments made by a Finnish viewer in an effort to clarify Finnish interpretations for American viewers of one scene in "Tango Finlandia." The following are her words beginning with a replay of the scene of concern to her:

> The American commentator says: It strikes me traveling around this country that people are terribly shy, particularly the men.
> The Finnish male replies: Among ourselves, we think that is the natural way to be, not to sort of stick out. It's easy to see that from coming from another country you think of it as shyness, and it probably is yes.

> My interpretation for the statements would be that we (Finns) want to protect ourselves from the unknown but we also want to protect the other person from the unknown. We want to respect the other person's privacy and in a way make sure that he/she really wants to talk. In Finland it's okay not to talk all the time and in my opinion most of the Finns don't feel awkward when nobody talks. We don't feel that we have to talk just for talking (in order to avoid silence) and we can feel comfortable when nobody is talking, we are comfortable with quietness.

The Finnish interlocutor explained further:

> When Finns talk about being shy they are simply referring to being quiet, observant and respectful of other people's physical and mental privacy. That is how our culture has taught us to be. Perhaps this is a natural way to be, to not stick out, but it is difficult to understand for people who are uncomfortable with silence. In Finland a person is respected if he or she begins with quiet respect of others and moves towards talking when having something of added value for others to hear. In the statement above Knutas is being polite. He doesn't agree with Safer but believes Safer won't understand the positive side of shyness among Finns.

The Finnish viewer has carefully presented a Finnish discourse, which can be used to understand Knutas more deeply. In order to do so, we must move beyond a simple gloss of Finns as "terribly shy" or "clinically shy" to an understanding of some Finnish conduct as being quiet, observant, private, and respectful. This rendering of course contrasts with the American discourse of Finns as inexpressive, shy, and sad. These Finnish terms provide a different set of dimensions and parameters for understanding Finnish ways. The US American discourse and its contrasts must be abandoned in order to peer through this Finnish window, or to walk through this Finnish door, to enter the Finnish discursive country. In the process, invoking the famous line from the *Wizard of Oz*, several American viewers often exclaimed they realized, now, they were not in Kansas anymore!

As mentioned already, the final "I love you" sequence (lines 316–353) serves as a puzzling part of the document for some US American viewers, for it can go particularly deep. American viewers can react by reporting that they often say "I love you" every day to their loved ones. They say they think they should do that and cannot understand why someone, like the Finns, would NOT do that too! "Don't they love each other!?" If such thoughts become an impasse, the Finnish practices and premises can provide a way out by comparatively analyzing the practices. How do they and we do it, and why do it that way? This question can raise important questions about the meanings of love (and its use as exclusively romantic, or not), the various ways it can be expressed (verbally and/or nonverbally), when it is (and should be) expressed, and when not. This can also raise more general questions about cultural conceptions of social intercourse and emotions, emotion vocabularies and emotion expression.

Consider the following comments made by another Finnish viewer. She is offering a deeper reading of Ms. Koriseva's comments in an effort to clarify the Finnish version of things. She is talking about this passage from Ms. Koriseva (lines 104–114):

> "We have like a wall here. We try to look at you and watch who you are—what you are before we dare to come to you and speak with you and I guess the American people are more like *hi—who are you. Where are you from?* Nice meeting you. I love you."

She says:

> Miss Koriseva is using the verb to dare, which carries a double meaning in the Finnish language. It can mean a lack of self-confidence. But here it means "We like to see who you are and what you are doing before we feel like coming to you." That means we want to come to you but also want to be sure you want us to come to see you. We don't dare to interfere with your privacy because we respect it, and we know that you expect us to respect it.

She implies further that the question, "where are you from," and the comments "nice meeting you" and "I love you" seem to be typical American sayings but from a Finnish view can often go without saying. As for the Finnish stance, here, it can create a watchful stance from which to act as well as activate great visual care before approaching others. These are not hindrances or deficiencies to sociable life as some US American viewers have said. They are deep Finnish practices of socializing, erected indeed upon Finnish premises of attentiveness, privacy, and respect. And, of course, these are different from another set foregrounded in a US American discourse where openness, talkativeness, and verbal connections are presumed to be good.

The part of the process we emphasize here is the use of comparative discourses to critically reflect upon one's own ways and as a way of learning something about others' ways. In the cases we have discussed, for US Americans, why presume verbal social contact, extroversion, happiness, explicit expressions of love, and the like are an unquestioned value? Similarly, for Finnish viewers, why presume quietude, verbal reserve, implicit emotion expression, and the like are an unquestioned value?

In what other ways might these practices get done?

This brings us to one more question we pose as a way of introducing our seventh principle: How might one's own ways and these other ways fuel intercultural misunderstanding, misattribution of intent, misalignment of motives, asynchrony of interaction, unproductive power relations, and the like? How might this be done better?

SPEAKING THROUGH ENRICHED CODES: OUR FINAL PRINCIPLE, INTERDISCOURSE DIALOGUE

At this point, we can make more explicit the larger objectives and goals at which we have aimed throughout this and similar projects. One is the description and interpretation of the ways different cultural discourses are active in and around human practices, such as a popular televised event—indeed, in this case, the most popular Finnish and American media text of which we know. Our descriptions and interpretations have produced an understanding of a large-scale social process we have anchored in the "Tango Finlandia" text and two of the cultural discourses in which it gains sense and meanings. There are other discourses we have not considered here but have explored. These include Austrian, British, French, German, Puerto Rican, Russian, and Swedish discourses, among others, which have seen and spoken about this text. One essential goal is discovering and understanding what various peoples have seen and said about this and other sociocultural practices—and to understand why they have THAT to say about it.

Another objective is an ideal toward which we strive; it is an enhanced dialogue among cultural discourses that proceeds from the naïve contrastive bases noted earlier, past inverted evaluations, to a productively engaged understanding of the discourses through which other people are speaking. It is crucial to note as we have documented here that people are often quick to judge and slow to understand. But through the noted process, understanding is possible for some, and a productive conversation can at times be created. This involves moving beyond the dominance (of a language, a political body, or a military group, or even a joke over others) to an intercultural dialogue through which an understanding of others is ably demonstrated and, if possible, explicitly so. It is this value of productively engaged cultural discourses that we are trying to promote as a way of sustainable living in our multicultural and global societies (see Carbaugh, 2013; Carbaugh, Boromisza-Habashi, and Ge, 2006; Carbaugh, Nuciforo, Saito, and Shin, 2011; Sleap and Sener, 2013).

In our final chapter, we conclude by describing five elements necessary to consider when creating this kind of understanding within and among cultural discourses, especially when focused upon prominent practices as those in mass mediated texts, or in everyday genres as when reporting about others (e.g., routinely or in "the news").

NOTES

1 See Carbaugh, 1988, 1996, 2005 where cultural and political foundations of this American discourse are analyzed in detail; cf. Cameron, 2000; Katriel and Philipsen, 1981.
2 We have developed this concept of "space" in much more detail in Berry and Carbaugh (2004) (cf. Berry, Nurmikari-Berry, and Carbaugh, 2004).
3 We may be overstating the dynamic here in order to make our point.
4 A second type of inversion is also possible but less typical in our case here, as when contrasting differences give birth in a reflective way to evaluations of one's own cultural self as inferior (this being active in many interdiscursive scenes of domination—see later). In this latter sense, one negatively evaluates self as an inversion of other; one appropriates the other's standard of judgment, thereby negatively evaluating one's own cultural ways. A dynamic of this latter kind occurred when I first visited Finland in 1993 and a Finnish teacher said, "We don't communicate very well here in Finland." What was meant, I later discovered, was that "we" Finns do not communicate as easily and openly as Americans seem to do, and this evaluation of Finnish practices was being negatively evaluated by the Finnish speaker on this occasion.
5 It can also lead to a solidifying of one's own sense of things and be a rejection of others' views.
6 We note here that we treat theoretical stances as also, possibly, cultural discourses of their own, as when speech act theory involves prominent American premises about speech, or some versions of auto-ethnography may involve American premises about expressing one's self. Admittedly, the latter are active to some degree here.

Chapter 8
Communication Practices and Cultural Discourses
Five Basic Findings

We conclude with five basic findings that are focused on the cultural nature of mass mediated texts like "Tango Finlandia." As we have worked with this and many similar types of data, we have found it useful to formulate these reminders concerning the mass mediation of communication, whether conducted through technological instruments like a television or a computer and whether done through the human body through voice and gesture.

1) ALL COMMUNICATION PRACTICES, INCLUDING ELECTRONICALLY MEDIATED PRACTICES, ARE PRODUCED AND INTERPRETED THROUGH CULTURAL CHANNELS, CULTURAL MEANS OF EXPRESSION, AND THEIR MEANINGS

We started this book by discussing reactions to a televised advertisement in Tartu, Estonia. That advertisement was broadcast through a channel that was seen and heard as a revolutionary way of disseminating information. As such, the ad itself was understood as part of that revolution. Without that cultural and political framing, one cannot understand the shape and meaning of that ad for at least those people. Further, the sounds of the music, the geographic landscape, the words used, and the multimodal nature of the text was conceived of, seen, and heard in cultural ways.

Similarly, the prominence of the television program *60 Minutes* in the United States as a "news" documentary provides a frame for the "Tango Finlandia" document that others elsewhere may not share or may not see in the same way. Or, the frame for many scenes as "dark humor" was active within a Finnish discourse, but the frame was not shared by others elsewhere. Similarly points of culturally contrasting expressive systems included the discursive mediation of "love" or "a natural way of being" through gestures rather than words. Each contributed to intercultural misunderstanding in and about the text. The reason why was a difference in the cultural means for and the meanings of expression.

In another study, Russian televised communication was hearable to Russians as an instrument of the state, as the American host of the program found this to be nearly incomprehensible (Carbaugh, 2005). A developing literature makes the point in a variety of ways. The role of radio talk in Israel has been culturally analyzed (Dori-Hacohen, 2013; Hamo, 2006; Katriel, 2004), as has Amish and Mennonite views of computers and mass media (Kraybill, 1998), "new media" among Latinos in the United States (Leonardi, 2003), mediation itself (Vasilyeva, 2004), and cultural uses and interpretations of the Internet among Saudis (Al-Saggaf, 2004), to mention only a few. In each, it is not only the channel and means of communication being used, but the very cultural conception of communication itself that needs understood. The media, the means, and its meanings are simply NOT the same everywhere. Our theories and models, our practices and policies, must not presume as much (Carbaugh, 2008, 2017b).

2) WITHIN EACH CHANNEL AND MEANS OF COMMUNICATION ARE CULTURAL ACTS AND FORMS OF CONDUCT

In our research reported in this book, the cultural acts and forms of expression are now demonstrably evident. Whether one should speak or be silent is a cultural matter. If speaking, how and when one should initiate such an act, and what it means to do so, all of these are cultural actions, cultural forms of expression. Similarly, at another level, the genre of the "Tango Finlandia" broadcast was presumably a "news" item to US American viewers. Even if suspicious of it, they assessed it as generally trustworthy and accurate. Finnish viewers, surprisingly so to us, also assessed the broadcast or parts of it as similarly accurate. Both were at an average of 3 on a 5 five-point scale. However, US American viewers assumed the broadcast was in the form of a "documentary" about Finland. Finnish viewers, if laughing at first at the "humor," by the end asked: What is the point of this kind of broadcast? Is it a "mockumentary"? In other words, the cultural actions reported and recounted during the broadcast made the form of the document unclear to all by the end. What action has the program done, and in what generic form is it? Even while numerically similar in assessments of its accuracy, responses concerning cultural actions and the overall form of communication varied dramatically—as is evident in our previous analyses.

As developed in Chapter 5, we believe that many Finnish viewers see this document, in the end, as a badly misfired joke. Knutas in particular was really funny especially to male Finnish viewers, as many Finnish viewers said, and they did see this also as quite humorous, but many were fearful, by the end, that US Americans simply do not get that parts of this report were indeed a joke. Our research supports the Finnish viewers' concern. As a result of this concern, then, what kind of document is this to Finnish viewers? Perhaps it is a form of "black humor." But knowingly it is not that to others, and thus not wholly to them. What is it to US American viewers? Perhaps it is a news documentary. But if so, it includes joking performances, exaggerations, caricatures, and so on, which were neither noticed nor understood by viewers in the United States as such. If this was created knowingly by a news program, it is a violation of common journalistic standards. Our reply has been to analyze it as we have and point again to the misunderstanding and negative cultural stereotypes that result from the performance—and eventually to propose ways to open some doors of remedy.

3) CULTURAL TERMS PROVIDE ACCESS TO LOCAL FRAMES FOR SPEAKING IN/ABOUT COMMUNICATIVE MEDIA, AND THESE MUST BE EXPLORED ATTENTIVELY IN INTERCULTURAL OR INTERNATIONAL CHANNELS

Our interpretation of this program was aided immeasurably when a Finnish viewer claimed, this is "black humor," or in Finnish "musta huumori". At the same time, we were viewing our video data of Finnish viewers watching and were humored by the degree to which a group of Finnish males laughed at it. Eventually, we were given a way of framing the document, crucial parts of the document, which opened cultural doors for us. Similarly, as we explored the Finnish language in the document and that Finns used to describe the document, we began hearing phrases repeated, emphasized, and claimed as important in understanding what this was all about. Our analyses throughout, in the transcript itself, and in Chapters 5 and 6 in particular illustrate, we hope, the utility, productivity, and necessity of explicitly exploring cultural terms in the language deemed significant and important to viewers. This is indispensable to good cultural discourse analyses. This is partly what is missing in many such reports, stuck as they are in phase one of the process we described in the previous chapter.

4) THE "SAME" IMAGES, SOUNDS, OR WORDS CAN CARRY DIFFERENT MEANINGS AND VALUES IN DIFFERENT CULTURAL DISCOURSES

At times in the course of this study, we have heard viewers point to the screen and say in exasperation, "It's right there in front of you, for everyone to see"! Our point complicates this reaction. One's cultural discourse situates one not just to say things differently, but to see things differently as well. "Tango Finlandia" includes footage of reindeer, a sauna scene, and tango halls, none of which are seen, in a deep sense, similarly by US American and Finnish viewers. The ways some Finns hold their faces in public were reported as central visual scenes repeatedly by US American viewers, but not by Finnish viewers. Some male Finnish viewers noted Knutas' Finnish "lip smack" early in the document; not once was this mentioned by a US American viewer. Our point is simply that the "same" visual document is, in an important sense, from the vantage of cultural discourse theory not the same document to one as it is to another. What is deemed a central image, what it means, which are focal and memorable, which were not noticed, all of this varies by cultural stance. Any analyst of the media, communication, or conversation who does not start with this basic point explicitly risks unknowingly supplying one's own cultural frame around the matter and thus skewing one's seeing and speaking about it in that direction.

5) AS WE DISCUSSED IN CHAPTER 1, A CULTURAL DISCOURSE IS COMPOSED OF HISTORICALLY TRANSMITTED SYSTEMS OF SYMBOLS (VERBAL, VISUAL, AURAL), SYMBOLIC FORMS, NORMS, FORMS OF COMMUNICATION, AND THEIR MEANINGS, WITH THESE MEANINGS INCLUDING EXPLICIT, AND IMPLICIT, COMMENTARY ABOUT ACTION, PERSONHOOD, SOCIAL RELATIONS, AND EMOTIONS

We have analyzed cultural discourses as they largely embrace and animate technologically and humanly mediated communication. We have understood a cultural discourse to be a distinctive expressive system, with its own history, including its ways of using the media, verbal and nonverbal means of communication, its symbolic terms, acts, forms, images, and rules. We have demonstrated the utility—we hope—of such analysis by examining what is likely the most popular Finnish and American text ever, the *60 Minutes* documentary entitled "Tango Finlandia." In the process, we hope to have shown how this communication involves a dual echoing structure, the simultaneous play of parallel voices, and the distinctive cultural forms of each, while being both produced and interpreted. We have formulated a way of understanding this intercultural discourse process at one level very specifically, at another quite generally, and have proposed ways of moving beyond the problems of misunderstandings, stereotyping, and domination to an engaged dialogue that understands such differences justly.

Intercultural dynamics such as these are increasingly prominent in our global and multicultural worlds. We must seek to understand better what is at stake in them so to better converse not only one's own way, but one with others, one about others, through means that productively engage each in their own terms, for it is through other worlds, inevitably, that our future lives together will gain their shape and meaning.

Appendix

Methodology
An Electronic Text and Its Cultural Discourses

The discursive terrain of concern to this study is broad and deep. We treat snippets of discourse as always already part of a cultural discourse. It is that, or eventually those, cultural discourses that provide perspective for noticing and rendering what we see and what we say about what we see. This is crucially important not just as a condition for practical living, but also in this book as our theoretical stance. We believe no one comes to a datum like a snippet of visual and verbal discourse as a blank slate; each such snippet is seen and heard from the perspective of some cultural stance(s), and it is that stance and those stances that we understand to be cultural discourses. Discursive data, then, are always, for people, already part of a larger discursive field, which leads us to see and hear and feel and to report what we see and hear and feel the way that we do.

The data of central concern for this study are of several kinds. The previous chapters introduced in detail the specific television program of main concern to us. The sounds, images, and languages of that document have been a source of data for us. A full transcript is thus included in Chapter 2. Yet again, we treat these data as organically part of larger cultural discourses of which they are inevitably a part.

A second source of data consists of viewers' first impressions recorded in writing immediately after viewing the broadcast. We have collected approximately 1,200 of these from viewers in the United States since the fall of 1993; we have collected approximately 500 of these from viewers in Finland over the same period. All viewers—from both countries—were recipients of a university education and varied in age from 18 to 64 years.

For purposes of this research and our teaching, we also orchestrated a kind of co-interviewing process between viewers in both countries. In other words, we collected questions from viewers in each country that they wanted to ask viewers in the other country after watching the television program. These questions were used to begin an intercultural discussion, including some detailed interviewing of viewers in one country by those in the other after the broadcast. We have recorded these questions, and the subsequent discussions, which occurred

APPENDIX: METHODOLOGY

largely in classrooms but also through a variety of email exchanges and video teleconferences.

In addition to these data, we have a large pool of more data. These include reactions of viewers in both countries to the discussions about the broadcast, viewers' efforts to see and speak about the broadcast from the vantage of the other, and viewers' efforts to rewrite parts of the broadcast in ways that better capture their eventual understanding of what was said in the original broadcast from their cultural perspective. These data are parts of the research project, which are essentially exercises in critical study, good ethnography, and/or applied journalism.

Our data were analyzed in several stages. A first phase of analysis involved creating transcripts that were attentive to the dynamics viewers saw and discussed as relevant in the program. The outcome of this process and details of these appear in Chapter 2. We will note here that the process of transcribing could not be separated from the cultural discourse analyses. Parts of the televised text were made relevant in one discourse, or the other, or others, which then led us back to the transcript to ensure this gesture, that vocalization, another space, image, intonation, or sequence, and so on was transcribed. In this sense, we have found the transcription process to be, knowingly or not, deeply tied to cultural discourses of analysts and participants alike. Again, the point we are making here is both a practical one and a theoretical one; we take the making of the transcript to be inevitably tied to eventual cultural ways of seeing/hearing patterns that are products of inquiry.

Just one example of this sort of process appears on line 43 of the transcript where Jan Knutas is recorded as producing a "lip smack." This sort of gestural sound was not recorded initially in our transcription. It was missed, or deemed not relevant if seen, or rendered uninteresting for present purposes, and so on. So, how does this sort of detail become relevant to this sort of analysis? It was mentioned as important by a Finnish male viewer, as something not only noticed but worthy of comment. It is demonstrably consequential within some versions of a Finnish discourse, and thus we included it. The same point applies, in our view, to every word, line, and feature of the transcript.

A second phase of analysis focused upon the first impressions recorded by viewers in each country. These analyses included only those viewers' reactions, which were formulated in what we eventually came to hear, as prominent Finnish or US American popular codes. We have many other cultural discourses in our data. As a result, we cannot here focus on a Puerto Rican discourse (nor the Chinese, English, Japanese, or Russian ones we have also collected relative to these data, and so on) in the United States. Similarly, we will not focus on the Austrian, French, German, Italian, or Swedish discourses we have noticed in Finland as well (but see Berry, Carbaugh, Innrater-Moser, Nurmikari-Berry, and Oesch, 2008). Our focus here is on a popular US American discourse (in Chapters 3 and 4) and a popular Finnish discourse (in Chapters 5 and 6). We do

103

so in order to treat these in detail. Our analyses of these discourses followed this procedure: it identified prominent statements and conversational moves made in the televised text by US American and by Finnish speakers; it identified what viewers recalled in the text about these statements and moves, eventually casting both as cultural stances about oneself and then about cultural others; it identified and used viewers' reports of memorable and potent visual images; these were analyzed as cultural accounts, yielding eventually cultural discourses of what was seen and reasons given for statements and moves. The findings from these analyses identified focal cultural terms, sequences, and premises reported later.

Through these first phases of analysis, we realized that viewers were treating the televised broadcast with references to strips of real-world behavior. In other words, the discursive scope viewers used to see and speak about the document included discursive links to other nonbroadcast, everyday practices and its various features. For this reason, we monitored in our data references and links to these practices and anecdotes about them, as these were used to make sense of the document itself. The chapters, especially Chapter 6, then, include parts of our larger corpus of field data that illustrate how the broadcast document is, as a result, a functional part of a larger discourse of social scenes, different normative preferences, histories, and political circumstances. By attending this way to viewers' accounts, we built the larger cultural discourses that were being used to see and speak about the broadcast. This involved analyzing focal terms in English and Finnish; the ways the semantic space of these terms varied in each language; the way each presumed a social situation or event; and the way each structured persons, actions, and feelings in intercultural encounters. Details of the framework used in these analyses are discussed in detail elsewhere (Berry, Nurmikari-Berry, and Carbaugh, 2004; Carbaugh, 1990, 151–175, 2005, 2007a, 2007b; Carbaugh and Cerulli, 2013; Philipsen, 1997, 2002; Scollo, 2011).

The prior analyses led down several paths: one is wide and deep, involving pedagogical lessons from this long cooperation between nations, teachers, and students. Some of these lessons have been reported elsewhere (Carbaugh and Berry, 2001). A second path involves a model of intercultural communication that has several objectives. One is the rendering of cultural discourses, especially in good journalistic reporting, as they are indeed being used in the world; a second is a better understanding of intercultural dynamics as they are active in televised and everyday encounters; a third is a better understanding of cultural learning, competence, and adaptation within intercultural processes, with special attention to the possible transitioning between cultural discourses. Some of these lessons are presented in our seventh and eighth chapters.

References

Aakhus, Mark. (2001). Technocratic and design stances toward communication expertise: How GDSS facilitators understand their work. *Journal of Applied Communication Research*, 29, 341–371.

Al-Saggaf, Yeslam. (2004). The effect of online community on offline community in Saudi Arabia. *The Electronic Journal on Information Systems in Developing Countries*, 16, 1–16.

Bailey, Benjamin. (2000). Communicative behavior and conflict between African American customers and Korean immigrant retailers in Los Angeles. *Discourse & Society*, 11, 86–108.

Basso, Keith H. (1979). *Portraits of "the Whiteman": Linguistic Play and Cultural Symbols among the Western Apache*. Cambridge, UK: Cambridge University Press.

Baxter, Leslie. (1993). "Talking things through" and "putting it in writing": Two codes of communication in an academic institution. *Journal of Applied Communication Research*, 21, 313–326.

Baxter, Leslie and Daena Goldsmith. (1990). Cultural terms for communication events among some American high school adolescents. *Western Journal of Speech Communication*, 54, 377–394.

Berry, Michael. (1997). Speaking culturally about personhood, motherhood, and career. *Administrative Studies (Finland)*, 4, 304–325.

Berry, Michael. (2009). The social and cultural realization of diversity: An interview with Donal Carbaugh. *Language and Intercultural Communication*, 9, 230–241.

Berry, Michael. (2011). Communicating the cultural richness of Finnish *hiljaisuus* (silence). *Cercles*, 1(2), 1–24.

Berry, Michael, Donal Carbaugh, Caecelia Innrater-Moser, Marjatta Nurmikari-Berry, and Walter Oesch (2008). *"That's Not Me": Learning to Cope with Sensitive Cultural Issues* (ISBN 978-952-92-2540-8).

Berry, Michael, Marjatta Nurmikari-Berry, and Donal Carbaugh. (2004). Communicating Finnish quietude: A pedagogical process for discovering implicit cultural meanings in languages. *Language and Intercultural Communication*, 4, 261–280.

REFERENCES

Bloch, Linda-Renee. (2003). Who's afraid of being a *friere*? The analysis of communication through a key cultural frame. *Communication Theory*, 13, 125–159.

Bloch, Linda-Renee and Dafna Lemish. (2005). "I know I'm a *freierit*, but . . .": How a key cultural frame engenders a discourse of inequality. *Journal of Communication*, 55, 38–55.

Boromisza-Habashi, David. (2007). Freedom of expression, hate speech, and models of personhood in Hungarian political discourse. *Communication Law Review*, 7, 54–74.

Boromisza-Habashi, David. (2011). Dismantling the antiracist "hate speech" agenda in Hungary: An ethno-rhetorical analysis. *Text & Talk*, 31, 1–19.

Brockmeier, Jens and Donal Carbaugh. (2001). *Narrative and Identity: Studies in Autobiography, Self and Culture*. Amsterdam and Philadelphia: J.J. Benjamins.

Cameron, Deborah. (2000). *Good to Talk? Living and Working in a Communication Culture*. Thousand Oaks, CA: Sage.

Campbell, Richard. (1991). *60 Minutes and the News: A Mythology for Middle American*. Chicago and Urbana, IL: University of Illinois Press.

Campbell, Richard. (1993). Don Hewitt's durable hour. *Columbia Journalism Review*, 32(3), 25–28.

Carbaugh, Donal. (1988). *Talking American: Cultural Discourses on Donahue*. Norwood, NJ: Ablex.

Carbaugh, Donal. (1989). Fifty terms for talk: A cross-cultural study. *International and Intercultural Communication Annual*, 13, 93–120.

Carbaugh, Donal. (1989/1990). The critical voice in ethnography of communication research. *Research on Language and Social Interaction*, 23, 261–282.

Carbaugh, Donal (ed.). (1990). *Cultural Communication and Intercultural Contact*. Hillsdale, NJ: Lawrence Erlbaum Publishers.

Carbaugh, Donal. (1996). *Situating Selves: The Communication of Social Identity in American Scenes*. Albany, NY: State University of New York Press.

Carbaugh, Donal. (1999). "Just listen": "Listening" and landscape among the blackfeet. *Western Journal of Communication*, 63(3), 250–270.

Carbaugh, Donal. (2005). *Cultures in Conversation*. New York: Lawrence Erlbaum Associates.

Carbaugh, Donal. (2007a). Cultural discourse analysis: The investigation of communication practices with special attention to intercultural encounters. *Journal of Intercultural Communication Research*, 36, 167–182.

Carbaugh, Donal. (2007b). Six basic principles in the communication of social identities: The special case of clinical discourses. *Communication and Medicine*, 4, 111–115.

Carbaugh, Donal. (2008). Particularizing communication policy. The International Symposium on Communication Policy sponsored by the International Communication Association. Schoodic Peninsula, ME.

REFERENCES

Carbaugh, Donal. (2011). Codes and Cultural Discourse Analysis. In *Oxford Bibliographies Online: Communication*. Oxford, UK and Malden, MA: Wiley-Blackwell.

Carbaugh, Donal. (2013). On dialogue studies. *Journal of Dialogue Studies*, 1(1), 9–28.

Carbaugh, Donal. (2016). *The Handbook of Communication in Cross-Cultural Perspective: International Communication Association Handbook Series*. New York: Routledge.

Carbaugh, Donal. (2017a). Terms for talk, take 2: Theorizing communication through its cultural terms and practices. In D. Carbaugh (ed.), *The Handbook of Communication in Cross-cultural Perspective* (pp. 15–28). ICA Handbook Series. London and New York: Routledge, Taylor and Francis.

Carbaugh, Donal. (Ed.) (2017b). *The Handbook of Communication in Cross-cultural Perspective* (pp. 15–28). ICA Handbook Series. London and New York: Routledge, Taylor and Francis.

Carbaugh, Donal and Michael Berry. (2001). Communicating history, Finnish and American discourses: An ethnographic contribution to intercultural communication inquiry. *Communication Theory*, 11, 352–366.

Carbaugh, Donal, David Boromisza-Habashi, and Xinme Ge. (2006). Dialogue in cross-cultural perspective. In N. Aalto and E. Reuter (eds.), *Aspects of Intercultural Dialogue* (pp. 27–46). Koln, Germany: SAXA Verlag.

Carbaugh, Donal and Tovar Cerulli. (2013). Cultural discourses of dwelling: Investigating environmental communication as a place-based practice. *Environmental Communication: The Journal of Nature and Culture*, 7(1), 4–23.

Carbaugh, Donal, Timothy Gibson, and Trudy Milburn. (1997). A view of communication and culture: Scenes in an ethnic cultural center and private college. In B. Kovacic (ed.), *Emerging Theories of Human Communication* (pp. 1–24). Albany, NY: State University of New York Press.

Carbaugh, Donal, S. Lie, L. Locemele, and N. Sotirova, (2012). Ethnographic studies of intergroup communication. In H. Giles (Ed.), *The Handbook of Intergroup Communication* (ICA Handbook Series) (pp. 44–57). New York: Routledge.

Carbaugh, Donal, Elena Nuciforo, Makoto Saito, and Dong-shin Shin. (2011). Cultural discourses of "dialogue": The cases of Japanese, Korean and Russian. *Journal of International and Intercultural Communication*, 4, 87–108.

Carbaugh, Donal and Saila Poutiainen. (2005). Silence in third party introductions: A US American and Finnish dialogue. In *Cultures in Conversation* (pp. 27–38). New York: Lawrence Erlbaum Associates.

Carbaugh, D. and B. van Over. (2013). Interpersonal pragmatics and cultural discourse. *Journal of Pragmatics*, 58, 138–151.

Chick, J. Keith. (1990). The interactional accomplishment of discrimination in South Africa. In D. Carbaugh (ed.), *Cultural Communication and Intercultural Contact* (pp. 225–252). Hillsdale, NJ: Lawrence Erlbaum Publishers.

Covarrubias, Patricia Olivia. (2008). Masked silence sequences: Hearing discrimination in the college class room. *Communication, Culture & Critique*, 1, 227–252.

REFERENCES

Craig, R. T. (1999a). Communication theory as a field. *Communication Theory*, 9, 119–161.

Craig, R. T. (1999b). Metadiscourse, theory, and practice. *Research on Language and Social Interaction*, 32, 21–29.

Dallmayr, Fred. (1996). *Beyond Orientalism: Essays on Cross-Cultural Encounter*. Albany, NY: State University of New York Press.

Dori-Hacohen, G. (2013). "Rush, I love you": Interactional fandom on American political talk-radio. *International Journal of Communication*, 7, 2697–2719.

Duchan, Judith and Dana Kovarsky (eds.). (2005). *Diagnosis as Cultural Practice*. Berlin and New York: Mouton de Gruyter.

Eades, Diana. (2006). Beyond difference and domination? Intercultural communication in legal contexts. In S. Kiesling and C. B. Paulston (eds.), *Intercultural Discourse and Communication* (pp. 304–316). Malden, MA: Blackwell Publishing.

Fitch, Kristine. (1998). *Speaking Relationally: Culture, Communication, and Interpersonal Connection*. New York: The Guildford Press.

Garrett, M. (1993). Wit, power, and oppositional groups: A case study of "pure talk". *Quarterly Journal of Speech*, 79, 303–318.

Geertz, Clifford. (1973). *The Interpretation of Cultures*. New York: Basic Books.

Goddard, Clifford and Anna Wierzbicka. (2004). Cultural scripts: What are they and what are they good for. *Intercultural Pragmatics*, 1(2), 153–166.

Gumperz, John J. (1982). *Discourse Strategies*. Cambridge, UK: Cambridge University Press.

Gumperz, John J. (1992). Contextualization and understanding. In Alessandro Duranti and Charles Goodwin (eds.), *Rethinking Context: Language as an Interactive Phenomenon* (pp. 229–252). Cambridge, UK: Cambridge University Press.

Hall, Bradford "J" and Mutsumi Noguchi. (1995). Engaging in "kenson": An extended case study of one form of common sense. *Human Relations*, 48, 1129–1147.

Hall, Bradford "J" and Kathleen Valde. (1995). "Brown nosing" as a cultural resource in American organizational speech. *Research on Language and Social Interaction*, 28, 131–150.

Hamo, Michal. (2006). Caught between freedom and control: "Ordinary" people's discursive positioning on an Israeli prime-time talk show. *Discourse & Society*, 17, 427–445.

Hastings, Sally. (2001). Social drama as a site for the communal construction and management of Asian Indian "stranger" identity. Research on Language and Social Interaction, 34 (4), 309–335.

Huspek, Michael and Kathleen Kendall. (1991). On withholding political voice: An analysis of the political vocabulary of a "nonpolitical" speech community. *Quarterly Journal of Speech*, 77, 1–19.

Hymes, D. (1972). Models of the interaction of language and social life. In J. Gumperz and D. Hymes (eds), *Directions in Sociolinguistics: The Ethnography of Communication* (pp. 35–71). New York: Holt, Rinehart & Winston.

REFERENCES

Katriel, Tamar. (2004). *Dialogic Moments: From Soul Talks to Talk Radio in Israeli Culture.* Detroit, MI: Wayne State University Press.

Katriel, Tamar and Gerry Philipsen. (1981). "What we need is communication": "Communication" as a cultural category in some American speech. *Communication Monographs*, 48, 301–317.

Klinge, Matti. (1990). *Let Us Be Finns: Essays on History.* Helsinki, Finland: Otava Publishing Company.

Koivusalo, Markku. (1999). Still life—the aesthetics of Finnish silence. In *Finland: The Northern Experience, New Europe, and the Next Millenium* (pp. 48–53). Helsinki, Finland: Tammi Publishers.

Kraybill, Donald B. (1998). Plain reservations: Amish and Mennonite views of media and computers. *Journal of Mass Media Ethics*, 13, 99–110.

Leonardi, Paul M. (2003). Problematizing 'new media': Culturally based perceptions of cell phones, computers, and the internet among United States Latinos. *Critical Studies in Media Communication*, 20, 160–179.

Lucy, John. (1992). *Language Diversity and Thought: A Reformulation of the Linguistic Relativity Hypothesis.* Cambridge, UK: Cambridge University Press.

Nelson, Christian. (2001). If it sounds too good to be true, it is: A Wittgensteinian approach to the conflict literature. *Language and Communication*, 21, 1–22.

Petkova, Diana and Jaakko Lehtonen (eds.). (2005). *Cultural Identity in an Intercultural Context.* Publications of the Department of Communication, N. 27. Jyvaskyla, Finland: University of Jyvaskyla.

Philipsen, Gerry. (1987). The prospect for cultural communication. In D. Kincaid (ed.) *Communication Theory: Eastern and Western Perspectives* (pp. 245–254). New York: Academic Press.

Philipsen, Gerry. (1992). *Speaking Culturally: Explorations in Social Communication.* Albany, NY: State University of New York Press.

Philipsen, Gerry. (1997). A theory of speech codes. In G. Philipsen and T. Albrecht (eds.), *Developing Communication Theories* (pp. 119–156). Albany, NY: State University of New York Press.

Philipsen, Gerry. (2000). Permission to speak the discourse of difference: A case study. *Research on Language and Social Interaction*, 33(2), 213–234.

Philipsen, Gerry. (2002). Cultural communication. In W. Gudykunst and B. Mody (eds.), *Handbook of International and Intercultural Communication* (pp. 51–67). Thousand Oaks, CA: Sage.

Philipsen, Gerry, L. M. Coutu, and P. Covarrubias. (2005). Speech codes theory: Restatement, revisions, and response to criticisms. *Theorizing about Intercultural Communication*, 55–68.

Poutiainen, Saila. (2005). Kulttuurista puhetta deittaamisesta. [Cultural talk about dating.] *Puhe ja kieli*, 25(3), 123–136.

Robinson, Susan. (2011). Anyone can know: Citizen journalism and the interpretive community of the mainstream press. *Journalism*, 12, 963–982.

REFERENCES

Sajavaara, Kari and Jaakko Lehtonen. (1997). The silent Finn revisited. In J. Adam (Ed.), *Silence: Interdisciplinary Perspectives* (pp. 262–283). New York: Mouton de Gruyter.

Sallinen-Kuparinen, Aino. (1986). Finnish communication reticence: Perceptions and self-reported behavior. *Studia Philologica Jyvaskylaensia* 19, University of Jyvaskyla, Finland.

Sawyer, Michelle Scollo. (2004). Nonverbal ways of communicating with nature: A cross-case study. *Environmental Communication Yearbook*, 1, 227–249.

Scollo, Michelle. (2011). Cultural approaches to discourse analysis: A theoretical and methodological conversation with special focus on Donal Carbaugh's cultural discourse theory. *Journal of Multicultural Discourses*, 6, 1–32.

Scollo, M. and D. Carbaugh. (2013). Introduction: Interpersonal communication: Qualities and culture. *Russian Journal of Communication*, 5 (2), 2013, 95–103.

Scollon, Ronald and Susanne Scollon. (1990). Athabascan-English inter-ethnic communication. In D. Carbaugh (ed.), *Cultural Communication and Intercultural Contact* (pp. 259–286). Hillsdale, NJ: Lawrence Erlbaum Publishers.

Sleap, F. and O. Sener. (2013). In Donal Carbaugh (ed.), *Dialogue Theories* (pp. 67–82). London: Dialogue Society.

Suopis, Cindy and Donal Carbaugh. (2005). Speaking about menopause: Possibilities for a cultural discourse analysis. In J. Duchan and D. Kovarsky (eds.), *Diagnosis as a Cultural Practice* (Series in Language, Power, and Social Process, pp. 263–276). Berlin and New York: Mouton de Gruyter.

Tannen, Deborah, ed. (1986). *Discourse in Cross-Cultural Communication*. Special issue of *Text* 6(2).

Taylor, Talbot. (1997). *Theorizing Language*. New York: Pergamon.

Thorburn, Richard. (1993). Don Hewitt's durable hour. *Columbia Journalism Review*, September/October.

Verschueren, Jef. (1985). *What People Say They Do with Words*. Norwood, NJ: Ablex.

Wierzbicka, Anna. (1997). *Understanding Cultures through Their Key Words: English, Russian, Polish, German, Japanese*. New York: Oxford University Press.

Wierzbicka, Anna. (2003). *Cross-Cultural Pragmatics: The Semantics of Human Interaction*. Berlin and New York: Mouton de Gruyter.

Wilkins, Richard. (2005). The optimal form: Inadequacies and excessiveness within the "asiallinen" [matter-of-fact] nonverbal style in public and civic settings in Finland. *Journal of Communication*, 55, 383–401.

Wilkins, Richard. (2007). Cultural frames: Loci of intercultural communication in a CBS *60 minutes* news segment. *International Journal of Intercultural Relations*, 31, 243–258.

Wilkins, Richard. (2009). The asiasta puhuminen event. In R. Wilkins and P. Isotalus (eds.), *Speech Culture in Finland* (pp. 63–84). Lanham, MD: University Press of America.

REFERENCES

Wilkins, Richard and Pekka Isotalus. (2009). *Speech Culture in Finland*. Lanham, MD: University Press of America.

Witteborn, Saskia. (2007a). The expression of Palestinian identity in narratives about personal experiences: Implications for the study of narrative, identity, and social interaction. *Research on Language and Social Interaction*, 40, 145–170.

Witteborn, Saskia. (2007b). The situated expression of Arab collective identities in the United States. *Journal of Communication*, 57, 556–575.

Witteborn, Saskia. (2010). The role of transnational NGOs in promoting global citizenship and globalizing communication practices. *Language and Intercultural Communication*, 10(4), 358–372.

Witteborn, Saskia and Leah Sprain. (2009). Grouping processes in a public meeting from an ethnography of communication and cultural discourse analysis perspective. *International Journal of Public Participation*, 3(2), 14–35.

Zelizer, Barbie. (1993). Journalists as interpretive communities. *Critical Studies in Mass Communication*, 10, 219–237.

Zelizer, Barbie. (2004). *Taking Journalism Seriously: News and the Academy*. Thousand Oaks, CA: Sage.

Index

actions 7, 10, 65, 68, 76, 77, 78, 81–2n2, 87–8, 101, 104; cultural 99; Finnish 70–1, 74–6, 77, 79, 83
Alar 12
aloneness 73–4, 88; *see also* "olla omissa oloissaan"
Americans 4, 30, 34, 56, 87–8, 92, 95; as expressive 39, 70, 87, 97n4; as extroverted 64, 76; and humor 59–60, 62, 99; impressions of Finns 58, 61, 64, 83, 87–8, 89, as superficial 85, 90
asynchronous difference 87–8
Australia 4

Britain 14

China 3, 4, 67
Clinton, Bill 12
Clinton, Hillary Rodham 12
communication codes 5, 7, 8, 37, 67, 103; unwritten Finnish 77–8, 82n5
communication, genres of 4–5, 84–5
consensus narrative 9, 13, 35
contemplation *see* meditation
contextualization conventions 7, 10
contrast 6, 38, 39, 48–9, 50, 53n2, 60, 61, 64, 65, 83–4, 85–91, 94, 96, 97n4, 98
contrastive discourse 53n2, 86
conversational inference 7–8
Conversation Analysis (CA) 8–9

core culture 13
Critical Discourse Analysis (CDA) 8–9
critical pluralism 93
critical reflection 91–3
cultural communication, theory of 7
cultural discourse 2–10, 31, 35, 37–8, 40, 41, 48–50, 67–8, 81, 84–6, 88–9, 90–2, 93–6, 97n6, 100–1, 102–4; American 35, 41–53, 83–4, 87, 90, 92, 94, 95, 97n1, 103; Finnish 31, 38–9, 54–65, 69–70, 79, 83, 85, 90, 92, 94, 98, 103; moving beyond one's own 92; theory of 6–7, 101
Cultural Discourse Analysis (or CuDA) 8–9, 100, 103
cultural inferences 10
cultural others 10, 41, 45, 48–50, 83, 84, 86, 87, 89, 104
cultural stories 4, 9

dark (black) humor 55, 58, 98, 99, 100
de Tocqueville, Alexis 82n4
discourse, genres of 3–4
discursive themes 42–8, 88
Donahue, Phil 2
double vision 30–1, 34, 40

echoing sequence (sequential structure) 8, 9–10, 30–1, 33–5, 37, 40, 42–3, 49, 69, 77, 84, 101; definition of 33;

INDEX

examples of 31–5, 68–9; results of 35; see also problem-response-puzzle form
Emerson, Ralph Waldo 8
emotions 39, 44, 46, 54–7, 63, 68, 87, 90, 95, 101
Estonia 1, 98
evaluating the other 88–91
exploration 91–3

Finland 4, 5, 14, 15, 16, 18, 24, 26, 30, 34, 35, 36, 38, 41, 42, 43, 46, 47, 48, 49, 50, 52, 54, 56, 57, 58, 60, 62, 73, 77, 78, 79–80, 81, 82n3, 82n4, 85, 88, 90, 94, 97n4, 99, 102, 103; history 80
Finns 15, 16, 30, 36, 41, 48, 50, 54–9, 61, 80, 92, 94, 100; as attentive 95; as brooding 15, 16, 34, 36, 38, 42, 43, 52; dancing 20, 26, 37, 59; as honest 23, 87; and humor 52, 55–9, 61–3; as inexpressive 23, 34, 37, 38, 41–3, 44–6, 48, 51, 58, 63, 65, 83, 85, 87–8, 94, 97n4; and "natural way of being" 70, 80–1, 82n3; as private 17, 34, 36, 43–4, 49, 90, 94; as quiet 64, 72–3, 90, 94; as respectful 85, 94, 95; as sad 36, 42–3, 46–7, 48, 50, 58, 83, 85, 88, 94; as shy 34, 36, 37, 38, 42–3, 47–8, 50, 52, 58, 69, 83, 85, 88, 89, 94; as stern 14; as thoughtful 70, 71, 75, 79, 81, 83, 85, 90–1, 92
Flowers, Gennifer 12
focal images 5, 43, 48, 85

Georgia 6
Ghana 6

Hakasalo, Ilpo 23–4, 30, 35, 36, 38, 42, 43
Helsinki 15, 18, 20, 30, 42, 49, 82n3
Hewitt, Don 11, 12
humor 50, 54–5, 57–8, 59, 60, 65, 99; self-deprecating 58–9, 65; see also dark (black) humor

imitative jokes 60–1, 64
interactional styles 5
intercultural communication 104
intercultural process 84, 85, 104; principles of 85–96; see also asynchronous difference; contrast; critical pluralism; critical reflection; evaluating the other; exploration; interdiscourse dialogue; inverting self; negation
interdiscourse dialogue 96
inverting self 88–91, 96, 97n4

Knutas, Jan 16–17, 19, 22, 25, 27–8, 30, 31–4, 36, 38, 42–3, 58, 61–4, 68–70, 77, 92, 94, 99, 100, 103
Koriseva, Arja 18–19, 25–8, 30, 34, 36, 38–9, 42, 73, 75, 76, 77, 95

language action verbs 67
Lapland 30, 65n1
Lewinsky, Monica 12
Lewis, Jerry 52
love: expressing 19, 27–9, 31–2, 33, 36–8, 39, 42, 43, 45–8, 51, 58, 61, 63, 66, 84, 87, 92, 94–5, 98; songs 24, 36

Marlboro Man 1, 6
media literacy 4
meditation 74–5, 78; see also "mietiskella"
meta-communicative phenomena 67, 81n1, 81–2n2; "kenson" 68, 70; "pure talk" 67; "putting it in writing" 68; "sharing feelings" 70; "soul talk" 68; "talking straight" 68, 70; "talking things through" 68; "talk radio" 68, 99
meta-discourse 67
meta-language 67
meta-pragmatic terms 67
Mexico 3
Middle East 3
"mietiskella" 70, 75–6, 79, 80
Moscow 2

"natural way to be" 19, 34, 68–70, 76, 77, 79, 81, 82n3, 84, 93, 94, 98; *see also* "olla omissa oloissaan"
negation 49, 51, 83, 85–6, 87–91
nested conceptualization 8

Obama, Barack 12
Obama, Michelle 12
"olla omissa oloissaan" 70–5, 77, 79, 80, 90
other, the 5, 8, 10, 49–50, 85–6, 88, 89, 90–1, 92, 97n4, 103; *see also* cultural others; othering
othering 49

parallel voices 9–10, 30–1, 34, 40, 69, 84, 101; examples of 37–9
personhood 64, 65, 68, 79, 82n2, 82n3, 101
Posner, Vladimir 2
potent phrases 5, 85
privacy 16, 34, 38, 39, 43–4, 48, 72–5, 78, 83, 90, 94, 95; *see also* "olla omissa oloissaan"
problem-response-puzzle form 35–7, 40

quietude 71–2, 74–5, 78–9, 82n6, 83, 95; *see also* "olla omissa oloissaan"

radiants 7–8
reflection *see* meditation
rhetoric of astonishment 10, 41–2, 46, 88–9
Russia 2–3, 15, 80

Safer, Morley 15–28, 30, 31–4, 36, 37, 38, 39, 41, 42, 43, 46, 47, 49, 56, 57, 62–3, 68–9, 74, 76, 77, 81, 82n4, 92, 93, 94
sauna 17, 65n1, 100

Schultz, Teri 18, 21, 27, 30, 31, 34, 36, 37, 41, 57, 81
Shanghai 3
Sibelius, Jean 17, 65n1
silence 61, 66, 67, 71, 73, 78–9, 92, 94; *see also* "olla omissa oloissaan"
60 Minutes 4, 6, 9, 14, 30, 41, 48, 52, 54, 57, 98, 101; and consensus narrative 13, 35; format of 11–12; history of 11; as morality play 12; as "news biz" 12; reporters as detectives 12–13; as "show biz" 12–13; and truth 12–13; *see also* "Tango Finlandia"
social relations 10, 61, 63, 68, 79, 81, 82n2, 101
Soviet Union 1, 2
space: concept of 97n2; intercultural 85; mental/personal 72, 75, 79, 90; textual 5, 104
Spacebridge 2–3
speech codes 68
Sweden 80

"Tango Finlandia" 13–14, 41, 50, 52, 54, 58, 59, 67, 83, 90, 93, 96, 98, 99, 100, 101; as a term 20; transcript of broadcast 14–29
tango hall 20, 23, 30, 100

United States 1, 2, 11, 14, 41, 42, 43, 45, 46, 49, 50, 52, 54, 56, 59, 85, 88, 98, 99, 100, 102, 103

Varenne, Herve 82n4

webs of signification 89
Western Apache 60–1

For Product Safety Concerns and Information please contact our EU
representative GPSR@taylorandfrancis.com
Taylor & Francis Verlag GmbH, Kaufingerstraße 24, 80331 München, Germany

www.ingramcontent.com/pod-product-compliance
Lightning Source LLC
Chambersburg PA
CBHW051615230426
43668CB00013B/2121